Chiara Antonia
d'Alessandro

CHANGING EUROPEAN CONSTITUTIONALISM

THE ITALIAN SCENARIO

EurytionPRESS

Eurytion PRESS

Managing Editor: Jose Gomez

Eurytion Press

ISBN: 978-84-949222-8-2

How to cite this book: Chiara Antonia d'Alessandro (2019). *Changing European Constitutionalism: The Italian Scenario*. 2nd Edition. Badajoz: Eurytion Press

Second Edition (First Edition published by UMET Press, 2018).

Published by Eurytion Press, S.L.

Avenida de Elvas, nº 50, 06006-Badajoz (Spain)

Summary

Introduction

According to the Dutch political scientist Arend Lijphart, despite the great variety of possible formal institutions, contemporary democracies can be said to follow two main models: those based on the majority principle and those based on the consensus principle[1]. In Lijphart's view, the majority principle identifies the majority of the population as the subject called upon to decide 'for the people'. The consensus principle also accepts the idea that the majority prevails over the minority but accepts majority rule only as a 'minimum requirement'. In fact, in consensual democracy, 'limited' majorities are not sufficient in themselves, and the aim is to maximise the actual size of the majority.

Lijphart explicitly states that he considers the interchangeable majority model a synonym of the so-called Westminster model, named after the United Kingdom's parliamentary form of government. And indeed, the whole British institutional system – starting from the electoral system known as 'first past the post', a strictly uninominal mechanism that tends to produce a two-party system –

[1] Cfr. A. Lijphart, *Le democrazie contemporanee*, il Mulino, Bologna, 2002.

gives maximum prominence to the 'majority' criterion at both constituency and parliamentary level, ensuring a high degree of governability regardless of the breadth of consensus that the government enjoys.

The choice of the Italian Constituent Assembly of 1948, however, was very different. Through the combined provision of a government with a strong parliamentary base and a rigidly proportional electoral system, the Assembly favoured the consensual model for the nascent Italian Republic. In fact, with the approval of the well-known Perassi motion[2], the Assembly opted for a less rationalised form of parliamentary government, with limited intervention on constitutional law so as to ensure the stability of the Government's relationship of confidence and its political leadership capability.

The Assembly, in the immediate post-war political and historical context, was aware of the need to sketch the contours of a new form of government for a society that had now become 'of the masses', so to speak, and it therefore made profoundly different demands from those of Liberal society and was radically opposed to those of Fascist society. In addition, 'the choice to become a Republic by the will of the people had effectively introduced a pivotal principle

[2] On 4 September 1946, after a brief but intense debate, the motion proposed by Tomaso Perassi was approved; it read: 'The second sub-commission [...], is in favour of the adoption of the parliamentary system to be regulated, however, by constitutional provisions to protect the requirements of stability in government operations and to avoid the degeneration of the parliamentary system.'

within the new system: that of the sovereignty of the people, to which it was necessary to give form and substance"[3].

Within the Constituent Assembly therefore, Calamandrei's proposal for a presidential system remained somewhat isolated[4], and the general trend was toward the establishment of a parliamentary system. What emerged clearly from the heated debate that preceded the vote was the concern of some of the more insightful members, not so much to create a new model of governance, but to provide adequate constitutional rationalisation mechanisms to ensure the governability of the country, considered a sort of primary value of (reborn) democracy, and the stability of government.

The idea was that the sovereignty expressed by the general will of everyone in the new-born Republic would be embodied above all, but not exclusively, by Parliament. It was essentially a matter of giving life to an institutional whole which, while accepting the centrality of Parliament and, albeit allowing various possible ways of exercising its central role, would maintain the balance between the main constitutional bodies, without letting any of them act without the control of the others, but distributing among Head of State, Government, and Parliament, the two major political functions of the State: the decision-making and the executive functions. It would do so in such a way that both functions would become the

---

[3] T.E. Frosini, *Forme di governo e partecipazione popolare*, Turin. 2008. p. 66, III edizione.
[4] Cfr. P. Calamandrei, *Costruire la democrazia. Premessa alla Costituente*, Milan. 1945

responsibility of each body, albeit in different proportions, at the same time ensuring that none of the three would be wholly excluded.

The Constituent Assembly thus set out to design a form of government that has been defined as 'rationalised parliamentarian oriented to creating balance'.[5] The element of balance is found above all in the intervention of the Head of State as a mediator in the classic dialectical relationship between the Government and Parliament. The same holds true for the mechanism whereby the Government is appointed by the president, combined with that of the bond of confidence between the Government and the Parliamentary Chambers; this is also the case of the presidential faculty to dissolve the Chambers in synergy with the President of the Council.

Although the choice of a rationalised parliamentary system was supported by the Constituent Assembly, what has emerged – partly due to the effect of a specific reading of a series of constitutional provisions, but especially a certain interpretative practice with regard to the Constitution itself – is a system marked by the clear prevalence of Parliament over all the other bodies, to the point that we may speak of a 'parliamentcentric' culture. In fact, it was mainly

[5] The first definition in this sense is probably by Vittorio Emanuele Orlando, *Studio intorno alla forma di governo vigente in Italia secondo la Cost. del 1948* in Rivista trimestrale di diritto pubblico, 1951, 1. In order to classify it, it may be said first of all that the form of government in Italy is *parliamentary*, but *rationalised*, and not only that; there is also a tendency *towards balance*, even if one wonders whether a process of rationalisation is actually possible. On this point, see the more recent R. Cherchi, *La forma di governo: dall'Assemblea costituente alle prospettive di revisione costituzionale*, in Costituzonalismo.it, 30/12/2008, 52.

the political parties of the time who wanted the constitutional norms, in particular those concerning government, to be as open and flexible as possible so they could be interpreted and supplement by the parties themselves and by the rules they would draw up.

Validation for this approach was found, first of all, in the formal composition of the text of the new Constitution itself, whose second part begins with a series of provisions devoted first to Parliament (articles 55-72), followed by those regarding the President of the Republic, with the provisions regarding Government coming last of all. This order does not appear to be random; rather it seems to aim to establish a hierarchy among the constitutional bodies.

The undisputed centrality of parliament is also due to the fundamental role of political parties since the collapse of the Fascist regime, as confirmed in Article 49 of the Constitution itself, which states that the parties compete 'by contributing to determining national policies through democratic processes'. It was clear then that the leading body ought to be Parliament, expressing a synthesis of the political powers, with not only the function of creating and approving laws but also, and above all, that of determining national policies. From this point of view, the Government, a far-from-central body, was responsible for carrying out what was established in Parliament.

As has been observed, there are two main reasons for this particular primacy of Parliament: firstly, the conviction that a democracy born from the ashes of a dictatorial regime should first of all be 'represented rather than governed'[6], i.e., it was necessary to guarantee a plurality of parties, something best expressed in parliament. Secondly, there was a need to assuage a concern rooted in the political class of the time, namely to create constitutional instruments capable of handling two actors considered difficult to control: the Government and the electoral body.

A constitution of this kind could also be the result of the decisive contribution of at least one other legal factor, that would, however, change over time: a strictly proportional electoral law guaranteeing parties representation in Parliament, even with a very limited and fragmented consensus among the people. The system also guaranteed the parties a chance to make their own choices for the purpose of forming a government, maximising the bargaining power of small and even very small parties only after the elections. In this context, the provision of confidence within parliament actually became a system whereby the Government was held 'hostage' by Parliamentary confidence, and Parliament, in turn, was held hostage by the political parties. In the eyes of the Italian people these were meant to represent the image of the democracy-driven State, and for a long time they actually they did so.

Substantially, the form of government in Italy during the so-called First Republic (from 1948 until the early 90s) was that of a

---

[6] T.E. Frosini, cit., p. 74.

'republic of parties'[7] which, with the members of parliament representing the parties, made and unmade the majorities and, ultimately, assumed the role of arbitrators of the most important link of the *foedus* between the institutions and the people, namely trust.

The foregoing certainly contributed, at least up to a certain moment in time, to keeping the system in place, especially given the loyalty of the Italians to their parties, largely based on ideological convictions. However, the crisis of the political parties that began in the 1990s and coincided with the crisis of the great ideologies after 1989, brought down with it the fundamental relationship of trust between the people/electorate and the institutions of the State.

Various courses of action were undertaken to try to remedy this unprecedented crisis. On the one hand, attempts were made to reduce the institutional role of the parties; we recall in particular the referendums aiming to abolish preferential treatment in the electoral process and the public funding of parties.

The lawmakers tried to adapt to the problem of the parties by attempting to make the system more directly governable, binding it more to the electoral vote than to the subsequent choices of the parties, by adopting majority (election laws 276 and 277 of 1996, the so-called *Mattarellum*) or proportional electoral systems with a bonus for the one with the greatest number of votes (the so-called Calderoli Law, no. 270 of 2005).

[7] See P. Scoppola, *La Repubblica dei partiti. Evoluzione e crisi di un sistema politico, 1945-1996*, Bologna. 1997.

Attempts at reform have had an even stronger effect on the text of the Constitution itself.

The following pages outline the Italian Parliament's most significant attempts at constitutional reform from the 1980s to the present day.

These attempts at introducing change mainly focus on Part II of the Constitution, centred on the description of the organisation of the Republic and the main constitutional bodies that make it up, namely the political and institutional heart of the Constitution itself.

In all these ideas for reform, which, as we shall see, have all come to nothing, the focus that emerges is the varyingly explicit strengthening of the role of the President of the Council of Ministers or, at any rate, the Government as a whole. A number of ways of strengthening their position have been presented: either through the suppression of typically Italian perfect bicameralism (the goal of all the bills and laws that were examined) or the introduction of a Prime Minister instead of the President of the Council of Ministers, a subtle but not insignificant difference. Yet another option was the attempted introduction of the constructive vote of no confidence, imported from other European countries. The goal was always the same: every one of these ideas for reform aimed to strengthen the executive branch of government.

Reforms of such importance would have, as we will see, affected what lies at the heart of parliamentary government, namely the relationship of confidence between the Executive and Legislative branches of Government, the essential relationship that, to borrow an expression used by Niklas Luhmann[8], can 'simplify' the infinite complexity of relationships, in this case political relations. A 'new' relationship of trust between these two constitutional bodies would have been created in almost all the models for reform that we shall be examining, not based on otherness and opposition but on collaboration; a collaboration made easier and closer thanks to the introduction of a single Chamber as the main political body.

Consequently, and more broadly speaking, these attempts to reform the Constitution would have affected the very form of parliamentary government in some way, favouring a *Government within Parliament*, one that would definitely have been stronger than that described in art. 92 et seq. of the current Italian Constitution.

The most recent attempt to revise it, the so-called Renzi-Boschi reform of only two years ago, upon which this essay will primarily focus, fits smoothly, as we will see, into the considerations we have formulated so far.

All these attempts have come to nothing, as we well know. Some, in fact, got no further than the presentation or bill stage, while others, like the Berlusconi reform and especially the most recent, the Renzi-Boschi reform, floundered at referendum.

What then are the reasons for these failures, considering that the need to make changes has been felt for many years now, and at-

[8] Cf. Niklas Luhmann, *La fiducia*, Bologna. 2002.

tempts to bring them about have been going on for more than thirty years? It is certainly too complex a question to answer here, but we can at least offer some reflections on it.

It is probably not, or at least not only, a question of the complexity of the revision procedure set out in Article 138 of the Italian Constitution. Nor is it a victory for those who argue that, in the minds of the people and their representatives, constitutional power has had its day, as the Constitution is, in fact, a catalogue of rights which, once recognised, exist once and for all. It is more probably a question of the inability of the political forces to coalesce around political majorities to gain more than a simple parliamentary majority in order to obtain at least the 2/3 of the votes of both branches of Parliament (under Article 138 of the Constitution) needed to finally enact the reform. At referendum, however, the electorate itself has always expressed a lack of faith in the reforms approved by the current majority, whether right or left.

What is certain is that at exactly seventy years from its introduction, the Italian Constitution appears to be unreformable[9].

Tancredi's famous words to the Prince of Salina come to mind:[10] 'If we want everything to remain as it is, everything must

---

[9] One case of rather incisive constitutional reform was that approved by Constitutional Law no. 3 of 2001, which was also passed at final referendum. It was the so-called Section V Amendment on the rules regarding Regions, Provinces, and Municipalities, making significant changes to the division of legislative powers between the State and the Regions in the Italian legal system, moving towards a form of federalism.

[10] A character in the well-known novel by Giuseppe Tommasi di Lampedusa, *Il Gattopardo*, 1958.

change'. In this case, it is a mere expression of willingness to change, radically reforming the Constitution so that nothing really changes.

CHAPTER I

The debate on the reformability of the Italian Constitution

1. 1.1. - *A rigid constitution, a reformable text?*

Institutional reform, and in particular that of a thoroughgoing reform of the Constitution, especially Part I[11], has long been a topic of discussion among the Italian public and scholars of law and politics, including the institutions themselves, especially those specifically responsible for constitutional reforms under art. 138.[12]

It would be impossible here to explore in any great depth the complex debate on the relationship between sovereignty and constituent power[13] or to give account of the very widespread, and in some way even pervasive, belief held by many exponents of political and legal culture in Italy and beyond, that constitutionalism is above all a matter of *fundamental rights*. These beliefs substantially,

---

[11] This is the part of the Italian Constitution dedicated to the description of the legal order of the Republic and the main subjects that make up the constitutional system, namely Parliament, the President of the Republic, Government, local authorities, etc.

[12] For an analysis of the attempts to reform the Italian Constitution over the years, with specific reference to Part II, cf. C. Fusaro, *Per una storia delle riforme istituzionali (1948-2015)*, in *Rivista Trimestrale di Diritto pubblico*, n. 2/2015, p. 431ff.

[13] On this, T.E. Frosini, *Potere costituzionale e sovranità popolare* in *Rassegna Parlamentare*, n.7, 2016 p. 7ff. From the political philosophy perspective, see B. De Giovanni *Elogio della sovranità politica*, Naples, 2015.

as in the classic forms of constitutionalism, see in a constitution 'the idea of a law that does not depend on even the strongest political power'[14] and precisely for this reason envisage the substantial autonomy of contingent political balancing forces.

In fact, according to the supporters of this view, the idea of the sovereignty of the people is misleading and dangerous in that, as the Italian constitutionalist Gustavo Zagrebelesky affirms, there was no twentieth-century dictatorship that did not claim to be legitimated by the people, all the more so for having been obtained by making lavish promises or by catch-all voting, ill-suited to expressing a true desire for popular government. The divinisation of the masses (*vox populi vox dei*) and *critical democracy* thus find themselves at opposing poles'[15].

The current thinking on this question on the one hand evokes the (to some extent) reasonable 'armouring', of the fundamental core of the Constitution as a charter of the rights of individuals and groups while also deeming it necessary to resist the 'lightness' of the political class in solving the problems of reorganising the political system with the all-too-easy evocation of various kinds of constituent *'powers' and 'stages'*.

Essentially, for the supporters of 'critical democracy', the only uncertainty is whether the notion of constituent power should be

[14] M. Dogliani, *Potere costituente e revisione costituzionale*, in *Quaderni Costituzionali*, 1995, 31 (that, albeit denying the legitimacy of a referendum being able to touch the heart of the Constitution, admits that the constituent power can do so).

[15] See G. Zagrebesky, *Il Crucifige e la democrazia*, Turin, 1995, p. 98 ff.

completely, and radically, removed from the arsenal of the juridical concepts of the constitutionalists, or whether it should remain but in a form so watered down as to become a limiting concept,[16] useful for purely theoretical purposes, but 'playing no part in the practice of constitutional law'[17].

More convincing, also because it is able to support the 'evolutionary nature' of the happenstance of human sociality, appears the thesis of those who believe[18] that sovereignty is manifest neither in elections nor fundamental rights and that it can very well be made apparent through even drastic reform of the Constitution, safeguarding some of the fundamental rights without which there is no constitution at all, since it ought to be understood as a fundamental charter of rights. If, therefore, the sovereignty of the people is 'an integral part of liberal democracy'[19], the fact cannot be ignored that according to the provisions of Article 138 of the Italian Constitution, the people, at any time and in their capacity as the electoral body, have the right to modify the current Constitution either directly or

---

[16] G. Silvestri, *Il potere costituente come problema teorico giuridico*, in *Studi in onore di Leopoldo Elia*, II, Milan, 1999, pp. 532 and ff.; more recently, A. Pace, *I limiti alla revisione costituzionale nell'ordinamento italiano ed europeo*, in *Nomos. Le attualità del diritto*, 1/2016.

[17] G. Silvestri, *Il potere costituente*, cit. p. 534.

[18] According to Paolo Rossi, rapporteur on the constitutional revision before the Constitutional Assembly, 'The Constitution must not be a mass of granite that splinters and cannot be shaped; nor must it be a flexible reed that bends with every breath of wind. It must be, should be, aims to be, of a kind of ductile steel that can only be reshaped through the action of fire and the hammer of a strong and conscious worker!'.

[19] T.E. Frosini, *Potere Costituente e Sovranità popolare*, cit., p. 8. The essay also contains an interesting excursus on comparative constitutional law on the subject.

indirectly. The Constitution did not, after all, emerge from the head of Zeus, but from a specific political will that was tasked, at a particular moment in history, namely the difficult years in the aftermath of the war, with drawing up a substantial catalogue of constantly evolving fundamental principles and rights, as well as with setting out the essential rules for life in the Italian Republic. These principles and rules would be valid at that time and for ever more until the people decided, in their constituent sovereignty and within certain limitations, to perform new acts of constituent sovereignty.

It should be remembered that since its foundation as a unitary State in 1861, Italy had been a constitutional monarchy governed by the so-called 'Albertine Statute', *octroyée* by the King of Piedmont, Carlo Alberto di Savoia in 1848 for the Kingdom of Sardinia, which would then become the primary unifying nucleus of the national State. It was a 'flexible' constitution, even adapting to the institutional upheaval of Fascism in the period from 1922 to 1943 during which it remained in force and co-existing with the racial laws of the 1930s issued in virtue of the Italo-German axis. After the fall of Fascism and the end of the war, it was, therefore, essential to set up new forms of political institution and, above all, a new Constitution.

The path towards the adoption of the new Constitution was particularly complex: the choice between Monarchy and Republic was entrusted directly to the sovereign people via the institutional referendum of 2nd June 1946[20]. At the same time, on that same day, provision was made for the election of the members of the Constituent Assembly[21]. Of course, the Assembly had the task of identifying the 'hard core' of the fundamental rights without which there would be no true democracy, but it also chose, among the many possible options, the institutional mechanisms necessary for a democratic state to function as contained in Part II of the Italian Constitution: these are sometimes very effective and sometimes less so. The members of the Assembly were certainly aware of the historicity and modifiability of these mechanisms, and therefore did not fail to regulate, through art. 138, the methods of revising the Constitution. However, they placed no formal limit on modifications except that set out in art. 139, which provides for the irrevocability of the Republic, evidently conforming to the only constitutional decision taken directly by the people.

[20] 2 June 1946 is a historic date in Italian history. Italian voters including, for the first time, women were called upon to choose a form of government for Italy in the aftermath of the Second World War and twenty years of Fascist dictatorship. Choosing between Monarchy or a Republic with 54.3% of the votes, and a margin of just 2 million, the Italians chose the Republic, decreeing the end of the Kingdom of Italy and the exile of the Savoy dynasty that had reigned up to then.

[21] The Italian voters also elected the members of the Constituent Assembly entrusted with the task of drafting the Italian Constitution. However, under Legislative Decree no. 98/1946, which established it, the latter also had other tasks, in part the same as those of a legislative assembly, such as expressing a vote of confidence in the Government, approving the budget law, and ratifying international treaties. The Assembly, composed of 556 deputies, met for the first time on 25 June 1946; the work on drafting the Constitution should have lasted 8 months but went on until December 1947. On 1 January, 1948, the Italian Constitution came into force.

Therefore, the limitation in art. 139 is the only formal and explicit limitation to the possibility of modifying the Constitution; however, it is a consolidated opinion in legal literature that the reformability of the text of the Constitution also has some implicit substantive limitations[22]. First of all, it is argued that the 'Republican form' referred to in art. 139 can only be the one identified in art. 1 of the Constitution, as if to say that the republican form in question must necessarily be 'democratic', where 'sovereignty is entrusted to the people'. According to a broad interpretation of this reconstruction, supported also in various decisions of the Constitutional Court, (see judgments 18 of 1982, 170 of 1984, 1145 of 1988, and 366 of 1991) there are also, among the implicit limits to the modifiability of the Constitution, both the supreme principles of the constitutional order[23], partially coinciding with the values enshrined in the first 12 articles of the Constitution and closely linked to the democratic character of the Italian Republic, and the 'human rights' in

[22] See, *ex multis*: F. Modugno, *I principi costituzionali supremi come parametro del giudizio di legittimità costituzionale*, in *Il principio di unità del controllo sulle leggi nella giurisprudenza della Corte costituzionale*, Turin, 1991, pp. 247 ff.; M. Dogliani, *Potere costituente e revisione costituzionale della lotta per la Costituzione*, in A.A.V.V., *Il futuro della Costituzione*, Turin, 1996, pp. 254 ff; L. Ferrajoli, *Democrazia e Costituzione*, in *Il futuro della Costituzione* cit., p.p. 315 ff. F. Gallo, *Possibilità e limiti della revisione costituzionale*, in *Quaderni costituzionali* 3/2013, pp. 709 ff.

[23] On the difficulty of conceptualising the 'supreme principles', and exhaustive references to the case law of the Constitutional Court, P. Faraguna, *Ai confini della Costituzione. Principi supremi e identità costituzionale*, Milan, 2015.

art. 2 that the Constitution defines 'inviolable' and makes explicit in the 'freedoms' of art. 13 et seq[24].

But how does art. 138 of the Italian Constitution work? What rules does it provide regarding reform? At this point, we cannot fail to dwell briefly on its content. The Latin origins of the word 'revision' are *'revidere'* and *'revisio'*, which indicate a process of review, updating, and correction; terms used in the past to refer both to the procedure of 'revision' and to the actual effect of this procedure. In this regard, it may be said that revision is 'the result of the procedure adopted to adapt an existing situation to the new order of things in which it is acting'.[25]

From a more strictly legal point of view, the procedure can be defined as a 'legal act through which a previous act is substantially re-examined in order to confirm, amend, or annul it'[26]. It is evident that a procedure of this kind, especially at constitutional level, affects already defined legal structures and situations, and for this reason the careful reconciliation of two opposing needs is required: on the one hand the fundamental requirement of the *certainty* of law, and on the other, that of *justice,* the only value that can be placed on an equal footing with that of certainty and even prevail over it in

---

[24] See Decisions of the Corte Costituzionale, n. 18 of 1982, n. 170 of 1984, n.1146 of 1988, n. 366 of 1991.

[25] S. M. Cicconetti, *Revisione Costituzionale*, entry in Enciclopedia del diritto, Milan, vol. XL, 1989, p.106.

[26] *Revisione*, in *Grande dizionario enciclopedico* P. Fedele (ed), XV, Turin p.841, 1971.

cases where justice is understood as greater attention to the situation and interests worthy of protection.

Specifically, the concept of constitutional revision can be said to come into being at the same time as that of the Constitution itself, together with requirements for the protection of the essential functions of a modern constitution, understood as a fundamental text situated at the head of the hierarchy of the sources of law, a Charter of Fundamental Rights and Freedoms, as well as an essential point of reference for the operations of every form of government. On the other hand, however, while respecting these fundamental functions typical of every modern Constitution, the revision process responds to the need for the Constitution to be up to date, evolving in line with a constantly changing contemporary society. Ultimately, the effect of the constitutional revision process is to allow the 'modification of the rules contained in the basic law of a State either because the underlying essential values have changed or because of the need to make the institutions more functional by adapting them to the situations that have arisen in the life of the community'[27].

In fact, every modern rigid Constitution[28] provides for a varyingly complex mechanism of textual revision that may range from

---

[27] S. M. Cicconetti, *Revisione Costituzionale*, op. cit., p.107.

[28] The classic studies on the theme of James Bryce are now published in Italy, edited by di A. Pace, *Costituzioni flessibili e rigide*, 1998. For an original reading of the traditional rigidity-flexibility dichotomy regarding constitutions, see A. Pace, *Potere costituente, rigidità costituzionale, autovincoli legislativi*, 2002.

minor to somewhat substantial revisions. The Italian Constitution of 1948 is defined as a rigid Constitution due to the complexity of the constitutional revision procedure regulated by art. 138, which establishes the method for adopting laws concerning revision with the sole limitation, as mentioned above, of art. 139, namely the impossibility of abandoning the Republican form of State[29].

Art. 138 can be considered bivalent[30] because it represents on the one hand the *cause* of rigidity, and on the other the *consequence* of the choice of the Constituent Assembly to favour a text that provided for an aggravated modification procedure. And it is precisely because of this second aspect that they placed art. 138 in Section VI of the Constitution, dealing with 'constitutional guarantees'[31].

This means that changes to the Constitution, whether by means of thoroughgoing laws for constitutional revision or 'merely'

---

[29] In this regard, extending our gaze to other European countries, it may be affirmed that the Italian Constitution is in line with the other Constitutional Charters that often explicitly include among the limitations to constitutional revision that of modifying the form of state of that country. This is the case of the French Constitution, whose fourth paragraph of Article 89 establishes, in fact, that constitutional revision may not involve an attack on the territorial integrity of the State. Similarly, Section 79 of the German Basic Law contains the so-called eternity clause (Ewigkeitsklausel), i.e., the provision making it impossible to alter the federal Länder structure of the German State, considered to be a basic principle of the structure of the State, by means of a constitutional amendment. The example of the Spanish Constitution, on the other hand, is different, making provision for the possibility of total revision of the constitutional text (Art. 168), from which it is indirectly deduced that no limits are expressed regarding the process of constitutional revision.

[30] Cf. S. M. Cicconetti, *Revisione Costituzionale*, op. cit.

[31] Indeed, the Constituent Assembly debated the placement of art. 138 in the text. Galeotti, (*La Garanzia Costituzionale*, Milan 1950), was against including it among the constitutional guarantees, convinced of the nature of the article as the presupposition for such a guarantee and not as an instrument; Mortati (Institutions of Public Law, Padua, 1976) was favourable however, and his opinion prevailed.

constitutional laws, are possible but only by adopting a 'more complex' procedure than that of ordinary legislative procedure, governed by articles 70 et seq., although in reality, the Italian Constitution is considered one of the 'easiest' to change compared with other rigid Constitutions[32]. It should, however, be pointed out that there seems to be no agreement among scholars about how rigid the Italian Constitution actually is[33].

Art. 138 reads: *'The laws revising the Constitution and other constitutional laws are adopted by each House with two successive resolutions at intervals of not less than three months and are approved by an absolute majority of the members of each House in the second vote'*. This is essentially a two-track procedure that requires approval by both Houses. The first one follows the same route envisaged, pursuant to art. 72, for ordinary proceedings. The draft constitution-

---

[32] Extending the analysis to the constitutional revision procedures of the other European countries, the Italian procedure is a cumbersome one, but not one of the most complex. For example, in both Germany and Spain, particularly high majorities are required for the approval of the text (2/3 in Germany, 3/5 or 2/3 in Spain depending on the minor or major 'importance' of the reform). In very many cases, the dissolution of the Houses requires the final approval of the text by the new ones, for example, in Greece, Norway, Denmark and Spain itself, for the most important reforms. On the other side of the ocean, the United States also has a complex constitutional revision mechanism in place, involving not only Congress but also the parliaments of the federal states. For a comparative analysis of the rigidity of the Constitutions and the various systems of constitutional revision, cf. S. Bonfiglio, *Sulla rigidità delle Costituzioni. Il dibattito italiano e la prospettiva comparata*, in *Diritto pubblico*, no. 1/2015; G. De Vergottini, *Referendum e revisione costituzionale una analisi comparata* in *Giurisprudenza costituzionale*, no. 2/1994.

[33] On the topic of constitutional reform in Italy, see, among others: J. Luther, P. Portinaro, G. Zagrebelsky (eds), *Il futuro della Costituzione*, Turin, 1996; M. Piazza, *I limiti della revisione costituzionale nell'ordinamento italiano*, Padua, 2002; P. Carnevale, *La revisione costituzionale nella prassi del terzo millennio, una rassegna problematica*, in Rivista AIC, 1/2013, p. 24 ff.

al law, in fact, must be approved by both the Chamber of Deputies and the Senate in an identical text, and since both Houses can make changes to the proposed law, this means that every slight variation approved by one of the two Chambers must also pass to the other Chamber, so that the text will eventually 'travel' between the Chamber and Senate (the so-called 'navette' system) until both have approved the same version. It is sufficient for the proposed constitutional amendment to be approved by a relative majority.

However, since this is a more complex procedure, art. 138 calls for a second vote that must be passed not less than three months from the first in order to ensure the broadest possible discussion. After this time, the procedure may follow two different paths, opening up two possibilities:

1. If the second vote passes in both Houses with a qualified majority of 2/3 of the members of the assembly, the law is *definitively* approved and only requires promulgation by the President of the Republic and subsequent publication in the Official Gazette.

2 If, on the other hand, agreement on the amendment is not so broad, an absolute majority is sufficient; in this case, however, the text is not definitively approved as it may go to referendum at the request of 500,000 voters, 5 regional councils, or one fifth of the members of a House. Thus, a law approved by an absolute majority is not promulgated but published directly in the Official Gazette in order to start the three-month period required

to call a referendum. Promulgation will only take place if the outcome of the referendum is favourable or if three months pass with no valid call for a referendum.

1. 1.2.- *The role of the constitutional referendum*

Essentially, the text of the Constitution safeguards conflicting demands: on the one hand, the need for any amendment to the broadest political consensus possible and thus greater than the government majority. At the same time however, in order to prevent small parliamentary minorities obtaining any sort of power of veto that would make it practically impossible to amend the Constitution, art.138 allows approval of an amendment of the Constitution by only an absolute majority, generally coinciding with that of the Government, without prejudice to the possibility of recourse to the ballot box.

In the latter hypothesis, the Constitution seems to leave the last word to the electorate, who can therefore decide whether or not to approve the amendment approved by parliament[34].

In this regard, it is important to remember that the validity of a constitutional referendum, unlike the popular referendum regu-

---

[34] For further information on the subject of the constitutional referendum in Italy, see, among others S. P. Panunzio, *Riforme costituzionali e referendum*, in *Quaderni Costituzionali*, 3/1990; G. Ferri, *Il referendum nella revisione costituzionale*, Padova, 2001; G.P. Fontana, *Il referendum costituzionale nei processi di riforma della Repubblica*, Naples 2013; G. M. Salerno, *I referendum in Italia: fortune e debolezze di uno strumento multifunzionale*, in *Diritto pubblico comparato ed europeo*, 3/2005, p.1316 ff.

lated by art. 75 of the Italian Constitution, does not require a quorum of voters, as a simple majority is sufficient.

Of course, art. 138 has shown over the years that it constitutes effective protection for the rigidity of the Constitution from ordinary legislative process, as well as remarkable stability of the provisions of Constitution over time, albeit not permanently. Comparison of the numerous plans to amend the Constitution submitted to the Houses with those actually approved, as we will see later on, reveals that they are very few indeed, and this would lead one to think that the Constituent Assembly created a truly complex process making it almost impossible to modify the text of the Constitution.

There is most probably, however, a different explanation that lies not so much with the particular complexity of the mechanism but in the way the Italian political system itself works. Governments that are often weak and the result of multi-party compromises often find it very difficult to secure even government majorities of the necessary proportions. It is even more difficult for them to obtain (in order to avoid the extreme uncertainty of a referendum result) opposition support for decisions of extreme importance.

Nevertheless, art. 138 of the Constitution provides ample opportunity to amend the Constitution.

Is it reasonable to say that if these opportunities – with all their appropriately cautious procedures – did not exist, the fundamental right of the individual and all citizens to be a constituent power would be compromised? May it be said that, if this were not the case, the Constitution would not be a constitution, because without a freedom so essential to a democracy, it would not constitute a Charter of Rights and Liberties? The answer can only be affirmative, as no history can be fossilised at a given moment along its course; the law can certainly affirm the occurrence of 'definitive achievements', but it is impossible to hypothesize fixed mechanisms, especially in the light of a scientific and technological revolution that constantly changes our lives.

Chapter II

Twenty-five years of attempted reform: from the 1980s to the early twenty-first century

2. - 2.1. - *The Bozzi Commission*

Throughout the history of the Italian Parliament, as we have already observed, numerous attempts to reform the Constitution to some degree have been made by Governments or individual parties, as well as through the presentation of 'organic bills' produced by special bicameral commissions.

Such attempts have been numerous; the most important and influential, at least in terms of proposals put forward, are those derived from the appointment and subsequent work of three bicameral committees![35]

---

[35] Among the activities of the Italian Parliament, the Bicameral Committees have a particularly important role; their composition must reflect both branches of Parliament on an equal footing and the various parliamentary groups on a proportional basis. The Constitution expressly provides (art. 126) for just one bicameral committee for regional affairs, however, while several others have been established with powers of control, supervision, and security, as well as those charged, as we shall see, with drawing up a draft amendment to the Constitution.

The first, the so-called Bozzi Commission, took place during the ninth legislature[36], the second, the so-called De Mita-Iotti Commission, during the eleventh[37], and the third, the so-called D'Alema Commission, during the thirteenth legislature[38].

The bicameral Bozzi Commission had the task, with consultative functions, of formulating proposals for constitutional and legislative reforms while respecting the institutional competences of the Chambers and without interfering in the procedures of legislative initiatives, or in complex and urgent matters, such as the greater autonomy of local government, the Presidency of the Council, and the new procedure for prosecution proceedings"[39].

The Commission examined a very large number of the issues mentioned in the final report, also touching on – unlike the subsequent bicameral sections – Part I of the Constitution on *Rights and fundamental freedoms*. Important proposals were also drawn up under the heading *The Form of the State*, on the reduction of the number of members in both the Chamber of Deputies and the Senate, as well as the establishment of limits on electoral expenses. The Commission also proposed that only the Chamber of Deputies

---

[36] The Commission chaired by liberal Member Aldo Bozzi worked from 30 November 1983 (first meeting) to 29 January 1985 (date of the final report).

[37] The Commission was first chaired by Mr Ciriaco De Mita, a Christian Democrat, and then by Mr Nilde Iotti, a Communist, and worked from 9 November 1992 to 11 January 1994.

[38] The Commission chaired by Massimo D'Alema worked from 5 February 1997 to 4 November 1997.

[39] Senato della Repubblica, Servizio dei resoconti e delle comunicazioni istituzionali IX legislatura, *La Commissione parlamentare per le riforme istituzionali*.

could exercise the legislative functions, with the proviso that the Government or a third of the senators could request, within two days of approval, that the bill also be examined by the Senate, which, within the following 30 days, would have to send it back to the Chamber with the proposed amendments. In any case, only the Chamber would take the final decision.

As for the form of government and the always central topic in any form of parliamentary government, of the relationship of confidence between the Executive and Legislative branches, it is useful to remember that the approved text established the reform of Articles 92, 93, 94, and 96.[40] In essence, although the Bozzi proposal maintained parliamentary government, it gave new weight to the relationship of confidence between the Government and Parliament, and the role of the President of the Council.

The new draft of art. 94 envisaged that the Chambers in common session express, deny, or withdraw their confidence (in this case returning to proposals already discussed by the same Constituent Assembly[41]) to the person of the Prime Minister, appointed by the President of the Republic, with the open vote of each Member

[40] These are the articles of Section III of Part II of the Constitution dedicated to Government, its composition (Art. 92), its formation after general election (Art. 93) and the delicate issue of parliamentary confidence in the Executive (Art. 94), and, finally, the criminal liability of members of the Government (Art. 96).

[41] At the Constituent Assembly, the Honorable Members Mortati and Tosato proposed that the conferral of confidence should take place in joint sitting. But this initiative was challenged as it would have meant that the representativeness of the bi-cameral system would have been changed, giving rise to an artificial majority; for this reason it was deemed that the request for initial confidence in the Executive should take place separately in the two Houses.

of Parliament. Contrary to the provisions of the Constitution still in force, according to the proposed text, the President of the Council would take the oath and present the Head of State with a proposal to appoint Ministers *only after* obtaining the confidence of the Houses. In the event of resignation due to some extra-parliamentary crisis, the President of the Council would declare and justify his intention to resign before a joint sitting of Parliament. Likewise, the President of the Council's power to revoke the nomination of Ministers, which is not currently provided for in the Constitution, would also have to be discussed, allowing the Head of Government to act by petitioning the President of the Republic.

The Commission's effort to remedy the main flaws of the perfect bicameralism typical of the Italian system thus appears evident: a) by reducing the overall number of members of parliament, b) by making the Chamber of Deputies alone the main body with legislative power, and c) by concentrating the power to grant and revoke confidence in a single and special body: Parliament in joint session.

This would have resulted in the empowerment of the Chamber of Deputies due to the numerical relationship between the members of the two branches of Parliament. Furthermore, the proposal regarding the vote of confidence would also have strengthened Parliament as a whole, given that, unlike the provisions of the current Constitution, no President of the Council could consider himself such, still less could he swear in or propose and appoint ministers, without having obtained in advance the confidence of the Houses in solemn joint session.

On the other hand, the proposal itself would not have failed to significantly reinforce the role of the President of the Council, especially in relation to the Government, as it is evident that in this constitutional framework, confidence would not have been granted to the Government in general, which would not yet have been ap-pointed in its entirety but to *the President of the Council himself*. He would, moreover, have been further strengthened with respect to his Executive by being able to propose, through the same procedure as for appointment, the dismissal of individual ministers without all the difficulties and delays of *moral suasion* or, worse still, the traumatic procedure of the so-called motion of no-confidence in an individual minister as currently provided for in the parliamentary regulations but not disciplined by the text of the Constitution.

In any case, the three volumes of acts of the Bozzi Commis-sion did not have, at least at the time, any normative effects, and for now they remain good material for historians of constitutional law[42].

2. - 2.2. *The De Mita-Iotti Commission*

The De Mita-Iotti Commission, coming into being through the same procedure as the Bozzi Commission, namely through two

---

[42] On the work of the Bozzi Commission: P. Armaroli, *L'introvabile governa-bilità. Le strategie istituzionali dei partiti dalla Costituente alla Commissione Bozzi*, Padova, 1986; see also A. Barbera, *Una riforma per la Repubblica*, Rome, 1991

different but converging single-chamber acts (from both Chamber and Senate on July 23, 1992) initially had multiple tasks, i.e., to examine the proposals for amendments to only Part II of the Constitution, to examine bills regarding electoral law submitted to the Chamber, and to draw up a comprehensive draft for the amendment of various sections (I, II, III, IV, V) of the Constitution as well as the systems for the election of the constitutional bodies. Subsequently, Constitutional Law of 6 August 1993, which entered into force on 11 August, tasked the Commission with drawing up a comprehensive draft constitutional revision of Part II of the Constitution[43]. The Constitutional law also introduced a constitutional revision procedure partially derogating from the provisions of art. 138 but limited to the draft amendments already assigned[44].

The reform project that the Commission presented on 11 January 1994 contained legislative proposals for the revision of nu-

---

[43] Source *Servizio dei resoconti e delle comunicazioni istituzionali XI legislatura: la commissione parlamentare per le riforme istituzionali*, www.senato.it.

[44] In fact, the constitutional law stated that the Presidents of the Chamber and the Senate would assign all the draft constitutional and ordinary laws relating to the above matters submitted by the date of the entry into force of the constitutional law (11 August 1993) to the Commission. The Commission would have examined the draft laws assigned to it in the relevant House. The deadline for the examination phase would have been within six months from the date of entry into force of the constitutional law, and draft laws accompanied by explanatory reports would have been presented to the Houses. Within 30 days of that presentation, all Members and Senators had the right to present amendments to the texts adopted by the Commission to the President of the House to which they belonged, which would have given its opinion within 30 days. After these deadlines, the Presidents of the two Houses were to adopt the necessary arrangements to include the drafts proposed by the Commission in the agenda of their respective Assemblies and to establish the date by which each Chamber would proceed to the final vote.

merous articles in the Constitution, principally entailing a wide-ranging reform of the relationship between the State and the Regions and the definition of new guarantors to protect the autonomy of the Regions.

As for the form of government and the relationship of confidence, the text approved by the Commission revised articles 92, 93, 94, and 95 of the Constitution to favour a form of neoparlamentarianism with considerable similarities to the so-called 'German Chancellorship'. The amendments, while establishing the necessary existence of a fiduciary relationship between the Chambers and the executive, introduced significant changes in this regard.

The new text of art. 92 of the Constitution stated that joint session of Parliament would elect the Prime Minister by an absolute majority of its members and even go to the vote more than once if necessary, with nominations by at least one third of its members. If no candidate obtained the required majority within one month of the first session in Parliament, the candidate would be appointed by the President of the Republic. If the candidate nominated by the Head of State were not elected, Parliament would be dissolved.

The elected Prime Minister would appoint the ministers and deputy ministers directly, and none of them could be members of parliament. On the possible termination of the relationship of confidence between the Houses and the Premier, the new text, borrowing from the German Basic Law in the new art. 94 – now also found in the Spanish Constitution – provided for the introduction of the *constructive vote of no confidence.*

In fact, Parliament could only express no confidence in the Prime Minister if he had indicated his successor in a clarificatory motion.

The De Mita-Iotti Commission moved, therefore, in the direction of strengthening the relationship of confidence in the person of the President of the Council in whom 'confidence' was actually expressed, in person, through a form of direct election by Parliament in joint session. The introduction of the constructive vote of no confidence appeared not only as a way of ensuring the rapid resolution of any crises occurring during the legislature and avoiding any institutional *lacunae*, but also as a deterrent to the vote of no confidence in the Prime Minister, in the absence of a parliamentary situation whose consequences were inevitable: the appointment of an *already identified* Prime Minister or the dissolution of the Houses.

Also in this situation, confidence (through the election of the Prime Minister) or no confidence would be granted by both Chambers in the solemnity of the joint session.

The work of the De Mita Iotti Commission too remains the object of study for historians and future reformers because the project for the early dissolution of the XI legislature[45] was not discussed, nor was it resumed in the twelfth.

2. – 2.3. - *The D'Alema Commission, aka the 'Bicameral'*

After further stages of study[46], a new Commission established by Constitutional Law No. 1/1997 was set up during the 13th legislature; it was also responsible for revising Part II of the Constitution. Massimo D'Alema was elected President on 5th February 1997. At the time, he was Party Secretary of the Democratic Party of the Left, founded a few years earlier, evolving from the old Italian Communist Party. This Commission has lived on in parliamentary jargon as the *Bicameral* par excellence[47].

The Commission drew up an important plan to revise Part II of the Constitution to create a form of government based on a semi-presidential system with the Head of State being elected directly. Biparlamentarianism would have remained, but with a reduced number of representatives (400 MPs in the Chamber of Deputies and 200 in the Senate).

---

[45] This was the shortest-lived legislature in the history of the Italian Republic, the last of the so-called First Republic. It lasted 722 days; President of the Republic Oscar Luigi Scalfaro dissolved the Houses on April 19, 1994.

[46] We recall the case of the Committee chaired by Sen. Speroni, Minister for Constitutional Reform, composed of a number of university professors appointed by President of the Council, Silvio Berlusconi on 14 July 1994 during the 12th legislature. For a reflection on the proposals of the Bicameral Commission and the Speroni Committee, see S. Troilo *La ricerca della governabilità: la forma di governo nelle proposte della Commissione bicamerale e del Comitato Speroni*, Padua, 1996.

[47] For a reflection on the contents of this constitutional law and the differences between the procedure for constitutional revision it contains and art. 138 Cost. cf. A: Di Giovine, *Note sulla legge costituzionale n.1/1997*, in *Quad. Cost.* 1/1997, pp. 381 ff.

The initial vote of confidence was eliminated: the Prime Minister would have had to deliver his programme to the Houses within 10 days of the Government being formed and without having to call for parliamentary confidence. Obviously, the old confidence vote would have been replaced by the appointment of the Head of Government by the President of the Republic in whom a high degree of confidence had already been directly expressed by the electorate who had voted for him. Article 76 of that text conserved both the motion of no-confidence and the so-called question of confidence on the part of the Government, but unlike in the current text, if the call for reform was rejected, the Government would have been called to resign.

The reform was an attempt to move beyond so-called perfect bicameralism and saw the Chamber of Deputies as the 'political' chamber. In fact, in terms of approving laws on a wide range of subjects, the Senate had the faculty to propose possible amendments to a text already approved by the Chamber, but only the latter had the 'last word' in the approval of the law. The Senate would have retained equal powers in the legislative process only in a limited range of areas (for example, civil and political rights, fundamental freedoms, national and European elections etc. ...).[48]

---

[48] The reform also envisaged a further, 'mixed', type of legislative process, in which the Senate would be supplemented in special session by representatives of local government. Draft laws in this area had to be transmitted for approval by the Senate, which would have deliberated in its extended form with representatives of the local authorities. If the 'supplemented' Senate introduced modifications, the Chamber

The proposal for a semi-presidential form of government was accompanied by a two-stage electoral coalition law and the distinction between bicameral laws and single-chamber laws, with the Chamber of Deputies prevailing in the event of conflict.

Just like the others, the D'Alema Commission, which had raised great hopes of success, came to nothing, first of all because of the presentation of a number of hitherto unheard-of opposition amendments, (42,000). In addition, the approval procedure gave rise to new political alliances that did not, however, reach the final approval stage, especially the last action that ultimately signed the death warrant of the Commission, namely the request, in the form of an ultimatum by Silvio Berlusconi's team to change the nature of the reform by transforming it into a Chancellorship based on proportional representation.

Thus, also the acts of the D'Alema Commission remained an interesting dead letter[49].

2.- 2.4. *The constitutional reform of 16 November, 2005 (the so-called Berlusconi reform).*

After so many unsuccessful attempts that never obtained parliamentary approval, the first case of organic reform relating to Part

would have the final decision in cases regarding electoral legislation, governing bodies, and the basic functions of Municipalities and Provinces, and the protection of essential national interests in matters entrusted to regional government.
  [49] For a thorough analysis of the Bicamerale, see Pegoraro, A. Rinella, *Legislazione e procedimento formativo della legge nella proposta di revisione costituzionale*, in Rassegna Parlamentare, 1/1998, pp. 17-53.

II of the Constitutional Charter to pass was the so-called Berlusconi reform, which finally made it at fourth reading in the Senate on 16 November 2005 but was rejected by the voters in the confirmatory referendum of 25-26 June 2006.

This was a complex text that maintained the two-chamber system, assigning to the Senate the nomination and tasks of the *Federal Senate of the Republic* in a cultural and political climate of 'Fiscal federalism', mainly supported by the Northern League party with a central role in the then coalition government.

The form of government was inspired by a reassessment of the majority principle. The new version of art. 92 stated that *'candidacy for the office of Prime Minister is the result of liaising with the candidates or with one or more lists of candidates for the election of the Chamber of Deputies (...). The law regulates the election of deputies in such a way as to favour the formation of a majority, linked to the office of Prime Minister'*.

The role of the Chamber of Deputies *alone* as the 'mirror' of the country on whose vote the election of the Prime Minister depends is clear. In this context, paragraph 2 of the new article 92 envisaged that 'The President of the Republic shall appoint the Prime Minister on the basis of the results of the elections to the Chamber of Deputies'.

The issue of confidence was not explicitly mentioned in the new text of art. 94, which made no express mention of a vote of trust, deeming that the vote of trust by the Houses was evidently covered, at least in part, by the election of the Prime Minister. The text only required the Head of Government to submit the programme and composition of the Government to the Houses (and therefore both Chambers) within 10 days of appointment. However, only the Chamber of Deputies would vote in favour or against the programme (without having to provide justification).

The new art. 94 specifically stated that the Prime Minister could call for a so-called *question of confidence* during his mandate, asking the Chamber to express its opinion with 'priority over any other proposal and with a roll-call vote'. Rejection of the proposal would, of course, have meant that the Government would resign. It should also be noted that, in envisaging a form of vote of no confidence similar to that of art. 94 in the current Constitution, the third paragraph of the new art. 94 introduces a new measure to prevent massive *side-changing*[50]. In fact, it was established that the Prime Minister would resign even if the motion of no-confidence were rejected but thanks to the decisive vote of deputies *not* belonging to the majority gained at election. In this case, parliament would certainly be dissolved early.

[50] In the language of Italian politics, the term *ribaltone* refers to a radical change in parliamentary alignment, where, to allow the formation of new government majorities, members of parliament elected for a specific party provide support to political parties that were opposed to them at the time of the elections. The term came into use in 1994 when Berlusconi's government lost the support of the Northern League, at the time part of the majority coalition, leading to the fall of the first Berlusconi government and the birth of a new one, chaired by Mr. Dini, with the support of the Northern League itself and the main opposition party until then, the Democratic Left Party.

The last paragraph of the new art. 94 reinstated the De Mita-Iotti Commission's *constructive vote of no confidence*, allowing the no-confidence motion to also designate a new President of the Council (with the obligation of the Head of State to appoint the President of the Council), but also in this case, only if carried out 'by Members of Parliament belonging to the majority in the Chamber, in compliance with the majority principle at the heart of the reform.

Lastly, art. 95 not only directly assigned guidance regarding government policy, but also the appointment and revocation of ministers to the Prime Minister.

The reform bill approved by Parliament (without a three-fifths majority at second reading in the two Houses) was submitted to a constitutional *referendum* for confirmation and was rejected[51].

Thus the 2005 constitutional reform also came to nothing

2.- 2.5. *Reflections on thirty years of failed reforms*

Some reflection on the attempts at reform examined so far would not be out of place at this juncture. An examination, albeit necessarily focused on the fundamental points of the proposals in question, highlights at least two points of particular note: 1) the perceived need to reform Part II of the Constitution, to which leading representatives of all the political forces have been committed in

---

[51] The result of the ballot was as follows: 25,753,782 total valid votes, 9,970,530 (38.71%) votes in favour, votes 15,783,269 (61.29%) against.

over thirty years since the appointment of the Bozzi Commission up to the most recent attempt, the Boschi-Renzi Reform, which we shall examine shortly, and 2) the extreme difficulty of reaching, in this regard, a text acceptable to all, a difficulty obviously due to the diversity of interests and opinions, not to mention the influence of the above-mentioned *critical democracy* school of thought, according to which the constituent power was already fulfilled with the approval of the original text of the Constitution, especially the first part, and the rights and duties it establishes: concrete possibilities for evolution and change in line with the unfolding of history.

Alongside this, however, we should also highlight the *problems* of the Italian constitutional system, some significant areas in the Constitution on which the official political class, Parliament itself, as *auctor* of the three two-chamber committees or 'non-constituent' legislator of the 2005 constitutional law, has constantly worked.

As far as the form of government is concerned, the key areas are principally bicameralism, maintained in all four of the projects mentioned, despite the various changes, but with a clear tendency towards the specialisation of the Senate as the Chamber for the Regions, and the greater weight of the Chamber of Deputies both in terms of legislative function, political orientation, and control.

Another topic is the number of deputies, which all the proposals aimed to reduce. Equally clear is the attempt, even more than in the current or proposed electoral system, to give greater weight to the majority principle, both in terms of *choice* and *decision-making*. This aspect emerges, albeit in different forms, in the various reform proposals examined here: the De Mita-Iotti proposal (for a 'Chancellorship'), but also, to some extent that of Bozzi and D'Alema, with the direct election of the President of the Republic, and last but not least, with the 'law' of 2005 which, albeit in a rather convoluted form, concentrated on a Prime Ministerial figure in some way emerging directly from the ballot box and, even more so, on the majority obtained from the same polls, the centre of political-constitutional power.

In all these cases, the parliamentary system was preserved and, with it, the *centrality of the vote of confidence*, albeit conferred in different ways, but seen as decisive, especially when negative. Greater focus on the majority principle in some cases led to the negative outcome of a specific initial vote of confidence: this was, for example, the case of the 'Chancellorship', where the vote of confidence was replaced by the parliamentary election of the Prime Minister in joint sitting. The 'Berlusconi reform' where the Prime Minister was – albeit not directly – chosen at the ballot box, was also a move in this direction.

Nevertheless, the vote of no confidence, even in the form of the rejection of the confirmation of confidence called for by the Government on a decisive measure, was still the moment when the Government-Parliament relationship would be sealed, so that the confirmed 'good health' of the relationship itself (through the vote of confidence/no confidence) continued to be an indispensable condition for its continuity.

It should also be noted that the reforms did not tend to focus confidence so much on the Government, like in the original Constitution currently in force, as on the recurrent figure of the 'Prime Minister' in the proposed reforms, unknown in our original constitutional system that famously envisages the somehow more reassuring figure of the President of the Council.

This would clearly have given a different and more incisive role to the Head of Government in relation to the executive, as the Prime Minister, and not the ministers acting collegially, and, still less as individuals, would be the figure obtaining confidence. As a result, in several cases, the Prime Minister would have the power not only to appoint (by means of a proposal to the Head of State or as a direct appointment in the case of the Berlusconi reform) but also to remove ministers.

.

Chapter III

An almost completed reform: the main objectives of the Renzi-Boschi constitutional law

3. – 3.1.. A government-led reform

We see, at this point, the evident difficulties that the various parliamentary committees experienced over the years in gaining final approval for any thoroughgoing reform of Part II of the Constitution due to the impossibility of reaching the broad consensus necessary for the approval of a new text, even with the inclusion of the opposition parties. Over the last decade, it looked as though it was the task of the parliamentary majorities themselves to promotes a now mature process of reform, albeit one exposed to the risk of death by referendum. Experience has shown, in fact, that proposals from Government majorities have not been able to garner more than the strict government majority (absolute majority) sufficient to allow a reform proposal to avoid the uncertain outcome of a referendum. This happened, as we have already seen, with the Berlusconi reform rejected at referendum. From the start of the seventeenth Republican legislature, the issue of institutional reforms to ensure a different form of national governance became paramount once more. In fact, when faced with very close election results, the President of the Republic, Giorgio Napolitano, failed in an initial attempt to form a political majority government, and in April 2013 Enrico Letta was given the task of forming a 'broad-based' government that would carry out incisive institutional reforms. The work of the Letta government soon came to nothing due to the fall of the executive itself[52].

A very different fate befell Constitutional Law 3/2011, better known as the amendment of Section V of the Constitution. Even though the law in question was passed by a centre-left majority (the Prodi Government) by itself, it also obtained a majority at the subsequent confirmatory referendum on 7th October 2001[53]. Perhaps in

[52] In fact, the Letta Government, following a plan agreed with the President of the Republic, followed two trajectories. On the one hand, in June 2013, it appointed a Commission for institutional reforms composed of 35 Italian jurists and politicians termed 'wise', acting as advisors to the Government in drawing up a draft constitutional law amending Part II of the Constitution. On the other hand, in June of the same year, he approved a draft constitutional law to set up a Parliamentary Constitutional Reform Committee of 20 Senators and 20 Deputies. The Committee, whose entry into office was subject to the approval of the constitutional law itself, would have been tasked with examining draft constitutional amendments, on the basis of the conclusions of the Committee of the Wise. The attempt to reform the Letta government was not successful, but the work of the Commission of the Wise was the starting point for the later Renzi-Boschi reform. For a more in-depth reflection on the attempt at reform in question, see: A. Anzon Deming, *La nuova strada per le riforme, non illegittima ma rischiosa*, in Rivista AIC 3/2013; S. Staiano, *Costituzionalisti e popolo*, in *federalismi.it*, 25/2013; G.M. Salerno, *Il disegno di legge costituzionale sull'istituzione del Comitato parlamentare per le riforme costituzionali e elettorali: spunti per alcune riflessioni preliminari*, in *Osservatorio costituzionale* 00/2013, p. 1ff.

[53] The law in question changed Section V of Part II of the Constitution (from articles 114-133) to the core, profoundly changing the structure of the relationships be-

the wake of the positive outcome of the reform carried out by the centre-left majority at that time, the Renzi Government (the seventeenth legislature), promoted the Boschi-Renzi amendment to reform Part V.

It is common knowledge that the Italian Parliament approved (at the last vote of the Chamber on 12 April, 2016) the constitutional law presented by the Government containing '*Provisions to move beyond equal bicameralism, a reduction in the number of deputies, the reduction of institutional operating costs, the closure of the CNEL, and the revision of Section V of Part II of the Constitution*'[54]. Since the majority that approved the law in the second vote of each chamber was less than two thirds of its members, the law itself, in accordance with art. 138, did not add to the conditions of exemption from referendum provided for by paragraph 2 of the same article, so that within 3 months of publication some members of parliament, from both minority and majority, made a request for a confirmatory *referendum*[55]. Hence, on 4 December 2016, the law *de quo* was put to a confirmatory *referendum* under art. 138, paragraph 2, of the Constitution.

This mechanism represented the choice of the Republican Constituent Assembly to draw up (thus breaking away from the Al-

---

tween the State, the Regions, and the local authorities, resulting in strong political decentralisation, tracing the outlines of a Republic of Autonomies.

[54] The law was published in Official Gazette no. 88 of April 15, 2015.

[55] For a lucid reflection on the eve of the constitutional referendum, see S. Traversa, *In vista del referendum costituzionale: luci ed ombre della riforma*, in *Rassegna parlamentare*, 2/2016, p. 159 ff.

bertine Statute) a rigid constitution that did not preclude the ultimate possibility of modification through consultation with the sovereign people via referendum. On the other hand, it should be recalled that 'the referendum is the institution on which the bond between constituent power and popular sovereignty is most firmly established, above all as a ratification of the new Constitution which, in this way, guarantees the Constitution itself a form of added legitimating value'[56].

Returning to the law in question, it should be remembered that the draft constitutional law was presented by the Renzi[57] Gov-

---

[56] T.E. Frosini, *Potere costituente e sovranità popolare*, cit., p. 25. The Constituent Assembly considered that a two-thirds majority in both branches of Parliament, reached through proportional representation, ensured a correspondence between the majority in Parliament and the majority of citizens. Only P. Rossi (in the session of 14 November, 1947) pointed out that 'in a country with a single-member constituency system, or where political expression is polarised around only two parties, a qualified majority of two thirds may not reflect the majority view in the country'. Indeed, precisely when a situation not unlike what Rossi had feared, i.e., a shift away from a majority or semi-majority electoral system, occurred, the condition of approval of the new constitutional texts by a qualified majority no longer existed, and it was necessary to call a referendum. This did not happen in the case of Constitutional Law no 1 of 20 April 2011, with which Italy followed up its commitment to the Treaty on Stability, the coordination and governance of the economic and monetary union known as the Fiscal compact, whose art. 3 binds the contracting States to balance (or reach a surplus on) budgets, which must be transposed 'into national law [...] by binding provisions of a permanent, preferably constitutional nature'. The legislation in question, involving changes to Articles 81, 97, 117, and 119 of the Constitution, was approved by a very large majority, even though it constitutes a clear and incisive phenomenon of the transfer of national sovereignty.
 The reform was provided for in the Democratic Party's programme and was presented by the Renzi government, which had effectively just taken office (22 February 2014).
 [57] The reform was part of the Democratic Party's programme and was presented by the Renzi government, which had just taken office (22 February 2014).

ernment on 8 April 2014[58]. It is not surprising, therefore, that the Government and the President of the Council were proud of having produced a text that had finally taken shape after so many years of fruitless attempts, with the result that the subsequent plebiscite was seen as a referendum in favour of, or against, the President of the Council[59].

3.- 3.2. *The Renzi-Boschi reform; imperfect bicameralism*

Let us now turn to the main contents of the Boschi-Renzi constitutional law and the overall design of the new constitutional mechanism. It may be useful to state from the outset that the main and most debated aspect of the reform concerned the abandoning of the so-called equal or perfect bicameralism of the Italian constitutional system. The law in question made several amendments to Section IV of Part I and Sections I, II, III, V and VI of Part II of the Constitution (in total 47 articles out of 139 were affected).

The main and most important change related, as already mentioned, to moving beyond perfect bicameralism in favour of a *differentiated or asymmetric bicameral system*. In the new arrange-

---

[58] On the same day, the Chamber, amid much controversy, approved the new electoral law, the so-called *Italicum*.

[59] See, among many: Nadia Urbinati, Renzi, *Il plebiscito per non spiegare la verità in* www.libertaegiustizia.it; 2016/04/25; P. Carnevale, *Considerazione critiche sull'iter e sulla procedura referendaria*, in *federalismi.it*, n. 12, 2016; A. Pace, *Le insuperabili criticità della riforma costituzionale Renzi-Boschi* in www.libertaegiustizia.it, 25/2/2016. For an opposing view on the same subject, see Adele Anzon Demmig, *Perché non convincono le ragioni del no al referendum costituzionale*, in Rivista AIC, n.2/2016; AA.VV., *Perché Sì, le ragioni della riforma costituzionale*, Bari, 2016.

ment, the Chamber of Deputies alone would have constituted an electorate in the political sense: it would have been elected directly through an individual, free, and secret vote – it would have become the only body to fully exercise legislative[60], guidance, and control functions over the Government, thus becoming the sole agent in the relationship of confidence with it.

The other branch of Parliament, the Senate, named in the original text by the Council of Ministers as *Senato delle Autonomie* before being renamed in the final text as *Senato della Repubblica*, would have mainly taken on 'a role of liaison between the State and the constitutive bodies of the Republic'[61] (art. 55 of the new text), and between the Republic and the European Union, playing an active role in the implementation of EU legislation and policies, as well as in assessing their impact on the territory[62]. The Senate would also have had powers to assess public administration policies and would have participated in the legislative function and in the assessment of its implementation.

---

[60] For a reflection on the changes to art. 70 of the Constitution envisaged by the reform, with particular attention to the so-called 'single-chamber' laws, see E. Rossi, *Il procedimento legislativo delle leggi 'monocamerali': prime considerazioni*, in Rivista AIC 3/2016, p. 171 ff. R. Bin, *Cercasi ragioni serie per il no*, in Rivista AIC 3/2016.

[61] On this, see R. Dickmann, *Appunti sul ruolo del Senato nel nuovo Parlamento repubblicano*, in *Federalismi.it*, n. 3/2016, p. 3; G. Brunelli, *La funzione legislativa bicamerale nel testo di revisione costituzionale: profili problematici*, in *Rassegna parlamentare* 4/2015 .

[62] A. Mastromarino, *Alcune prime riflessioni (sparse e brevi) in merito al progetto di superamento del bicameralismo paritario*, in Focus riforma Costituzionale, Federalismi n.5/2016, p. 4.

In terms of legislative procedure, the Senate would have participated equally with the Chamber in approving draft laws but *only* in a *limited* range of areas (e.g., laws pertaining to the constitution and constitutional revision, the ratification of international treaties, and laws regarding the organisation of the territorial authorities and their respective relationships with the State). In all other cases, the Senate would have had the power to decide, after the text of the law had already been approved by the Chamber, *whether* (on the request of 1/3 of its members) to examine the draft and make changes; if so, it would have had only 30 days from the presentation of the text to do so. In any case, the House of Deputies would have had the final say on any changes made.

Regarding the composition of the Senate of the Republic, perhaps one of the most discussed and debated points of the normative framework, i.e., that concerning the functions described in art. 55 of the new text, its members would have been elected from, and by, the Regional Councils and the mayors of their respective territories, except for five senators appointed by the President of the Republic. The number of senators would have been reduced from 315 to 100 members[63].

---

[63] More specifically, ninety-five senators were to represent the territorial institutions (and no longer the nation). They would have been elected by the Regional Councils and the Councils of the autonomous provinces of Trento and Bolzano; of these ninety-five, seventy-four were to be elected from among the members of the councils and twenty-one from among the mayors of the municipalities of their respective territories, with one mayor for each territory. Direct election would therefore have been replaced by a second-degree election by the regional councillors. As for the se-

The new text also introduced some changes to the mechanism for electing the President of the Republic (art. 83 of the revised text) and appointing judges to the Constitutional Court (art. 135 of the revised text). The reform also included the removal of references to Provinces[64] (article 118 of the revised text) from the Constitution, the abolition (article 99 of the revised text) of the National Council for Economy and Labour (CNEL)[65], and the deletion of

---

lection of the councillors, the text of the reform stated, in a manner that was not entirely clear, and referring to subsequent legislation, that the senators would be elected 'by proportional representation', 'in accordance with the choices expressed by the electors for the councillors on the occasion of the renewal of the councils' (art. 57 of the new text), and 'in proportion to the votes cast and the composition of each Council. The five senators appointed by the President were to be chosen from among the 'citizens who had brought lustre to the nation through their outstanding merits'. This is precisely what is prescribed by the current Art. 59, which, however, states that the senators appointed by the President are to hold their seat for life. In the new text, they would have held the position for seven years and could not have been reappointed.

[64] In the territorial organisation of the Italian Republic, the Provinces are the intermediate local authority between the Regions and the Municipalities. Article 5 of the Italian Constitutional Charter states, in fact, that 'The Constitution recognises and promotes local self-government'. In reality, implementation of this provision, which refers to a subsequent law to establish the principles, has been very slow, not only with regard to the Provinces but also other territorial bodies, municipalities and regions. Generally speaking, the legislative process establishing the functions of these territorial authorities came to an end in 2000 with the adoption of the Consolidated Law on Local Self-Government (Legislative Decree no. 267/2000), and with the Reform of Section V of the Constitution. From the second decade of the 2000s, however, a reversal began, dictated above all by the need for spending reviews, which led to a progressive reduction of the functions of the Provinces, until the promulgation of the so-called Delrio Law (Law 56/2014). The result has been a chaotic institutional framework in which, at the time of writing, some Provinces have been completely abolished (in some regions after a referendum, as in Sicily and Sardinia), while others have been replaced, under a law of 2014, by a new territorial authority, the Metropolitan City, and others still exist today, albeit with almost no powers. Despite this, arts 117 ff of the constitutional text continue to make express reference to them

[65] The National Council for Economy and Labour (CNEL) is a body of constitutional importance, envisaged by art. 99 as an advisory body for the Government, Parliament and Regions and can propose laws in the areas of economic, labour, and

the list of areas of concurrent legislation between the State and Re-gions[66] (article 117 of the revised text). Changes were also planned on the subject of referenda[67] (art. 70 of the revised text), legislative procedure, and use of the emergency ordinances[68].

Another significant change was the constitutionalisation of the call for a vote of confidence and the introduction of the so-called *fixed date vote* into the Italian constitutional system.

These are important innovations worth examining in greater depth.

---

social policy. For many years, it has in fact been considered a superfluous and unpro-ductive body, and its abolition had been on the cards for some time.

[66] The new text of art. 117 tried to remedy the critical situation that had arisen with the reform of Section V of the Constitution (2001), especially with reference to the many areas of shared competence between the legislative powers of the State and those of the Regions (more than 1500 disputes on conflict of attribution have been brought before the Constitutional Court due to questions of interpretation on the matter). The reform completely abolished the concurrent legislation by distributing the various areas it contained between the exclusive legislation of the State and that of the Regions; the latter were also left with residual competence in all other matters not specifically assigned to them. However, there was an important clause of supremacy which allowed the State to 'intervene in matters not reserved exclusively to legislation when the protection of the legal or economic unity of the Republic, or the protection of the national interest so requires' (Art. 117, paragraph 3 of the new text).

[67] With the new text of Article. 71, the reform would have provided for the pos-sibility 'to favour the participation of the citizens', and to call for propositive and con-sultative referendums increasing the forms of direct democracy currently provided for by the Italian constitutional system. The work of the new institutions depended on the enactment of a subsequent constitutional law that would have established its condi-tions and effects. For more details on this matter, see G. Ferri, *Il referendum popolare nella riforma costituzionale in itinere*, in *Rassegna parlamentare*, 3/2015.

[68] The most important amendment was the transposition into the Constitu-tion of the principle contained in a famous decision of the Constitutional Court, no. 360/1996, concerning the non-repetition of decrees not converted by Parliament at the end of the 60-day period set out in art. 77 of the Constitution.

3.- 3.3. *Confidence as a legislative technique and the introduction of fixed date voting.*

It is well known that the call for the vote of confidence, currently part of the practice of the Italian constitutional system (albeit not appearing in the text itself), now disciplined by the Regulations of the Chambers, consists in a declaration whereby the Government subordinates its presence in office to the outcome of a vote on a subject deemed, and thus declared, to be so fundamental to its political policy that the assent or dissent of one of the Houses on the matter can allow the continuation or cause the interruption of the relationship of confidence and the consequent resignation of the Government, should it be lacking.

The fact that the institution, arising from parliamentary practice in place at the time of the Albertine Statute, is not provided for by the current Constitution nor in the Boschi-Renzi reform, would not have meant that such a 'classic' institution found in some form in all parliaments regardless of any explicit provision would have disappeared. The institute in question constitutes, in fact, a Government 'counterbalance' to the possibility that the Parliament might, at any moment, remove the Executive by means of a motion of no-confidence, an institution specifically provided for in art. 94 of the Constitution[69].

---

[69] For further information on this subject, see M. Olivetti *La questione di fiducia nel sistema parlamentare italiano*, Milan, 1996; for a reflection on the use of the vote of confidence in the evolution of the form of Italian government, G. Piccirilli,

The question of confidence is, in fact, a necessary corollary to the bilateral and permanent nature of the relationship but also to the possible volatility of parliamentary confidence. Something bilateral and permanent but volatile must be accepted by both parties to the relationship.

It has already been mentioned that technical confidence has been, and still is, widely used by governments of the Republic (and not only of the Italian Republic) as a tool to *solicit* a parliamentary vote, as it can 'block' parliamentary debate on the confidence between government and majority, rather than the substance of the measure to be approved. The result is to speed up debate and also to *freeze* the text in the form proposed by the Government. This often becomes an *abuse*, especially with reference to the position of the 'call' regarding the so-called maxi-amendments possibly containing whole legislative texts[70] perhaps running to thousands of paragraphs.

In an attempt to remedy these abuses, which can also be linked to the need for the Government in office to be able to see an early outcome of its legislative proposals in Parliament at an early stage and in a manner corresponding to its proposals (except for res-

---

Paradossi della questione di fiducia ai tempi del maggioritario, in Quaderni Costituzionali, 2008

[70] See P. Pisicchio, *Dal Parlamento legislatore al parlamento degli atti di indirizzo*, in www.forumcostituzionale.it, pp. 1-15; for further details on the subject of maxi amendments and in particular on the degeneration of the use of this practice, see N. Lupo, *Emendamenti, maxi-emendamenti e questione di fiducia nelle legislature del maggioritario* in E. Gianfrancesco and N. Lupo (ed), *Le regole del diritto parlamentare nella dialettica tra maggioranza e opposizione*, Rome, 2007, and again, L. Cuocolo, *I 'maxi-emendamenti' tra opportunità e legittimità costituzionale*, in Giurisprudenza costituzionale, n. 6/2004;

ignations), the Government's first proposal for constitutional reform *de quo* sought to 'import' the *vote bloqué* of the Constitutional system of the French Fifth Republic into the Italian system[71]. Paragraph 6 of the new art. 72, as approved by the Council of Ministers[72], provided that the Government could ask the Chamber to decide on a bill within 60 days of the request. After this deadline (or another shorter one) the text proposed or accepted by the Government, and possibly amended following parliamentary debate, would then have been put to the vote 'without changes'.

The Government's proposal was, moreover, substantially in line with the Final Report of the last Commission for Constitutional Reform[73]; moreover, it seemed to meet the needs of contemporary institutional practices that have spawned the idea of a Legislator Government in international scholarship [74]. However, the proposal did not fail to raise some questions among scholars[75].

For some reason, the text of the new art. 72, paragraph 7, excluded the part on the 'blocked' vote that limited the possibility of

[71] Art 44 paragraph 3 of the French Constitution states, '*Si le Gouvernement le demande, l'Assemblée saisie se prononce par un seul vote sur tout ou partie du texte en discussion en se retenant que les amendements proposés ou acceptés du Gouvernement…*'.

[72] 31 March 2014.

[73] The commission established by the D.P.C.M. of 11 June 2013 in paragraph 2 of Chapter II of its shared report proposed that the Government could call for its own text to be put to the vote within a specific time, after which, the text proposed or accepted by the Government should be put to the vote 'without amendments'.

[74] On this point, see G. Caravale, *Il Governo legislatore. Esecutivo ed attività normativa in Gran Bretagna e negli Stati Uniti*, Milan, 2004.

[75] On this, see A. Ridolfi, *L'introduzione del voto bloccato*, in AIC Osservatorio costituzionale, 2014, pp.8 ff.

approving texts presented or accepted by the Government following parliamentary debate alone. In fact, art. 72 envisaged nothing more than a 'fixed date'[76] vote. But what did this mean?

In essence, the new paragraph 7 of art. 72 of the Constitution would have allowed the Government to ask the Chamber of Deputies to give priority to a specific bill on the agenda and for it to be put to final vote within a fixed deadline no more than 90 days after the Government's request.

Undoubtedly, the new text of paragraph 7 of art. 72 would have strengthened the Government's prerogatives within the legislative process as it would have allowed it to speed up the *process* of examination and approval of its own bills regarding the Government programme, thus helping to ensure its implementation[77]. This, it was believed, could have led to a reduction in the questions of confidence presented by the Government to bring about acceleration, namely cases of *technical confidence*, which was one of the main aims of the centre-left legislator. Some reflections on this are called for, however.

The transition from the 'blocked vote' formula to the 'fixed date vote' was certainly no small change, especially from the point of view of the desired reduction in the use of so-called technical

---

[76] This was in line with the proposal of the so-called Commission of Wise Men (established by President Napolitano on 30 March 2013) which established in its final report (12 April 2013), that the President of the Council could ask for a fixed date vote on the government's draft laws.

[77] See the dossier of the Servizio Studi della Camera dei deputati at *www.documenti.camera.it.*

confidence, with much more dubious results in terms of the effectiveness of regulatory intervention.

It is worth remembering that the 'French-style' *vote bloqué* is convenient for the Government and may constitute an alternative to the vote of confidence (also possible in the French constitutional system), not only as a way of speeding up the legislation approval procedure, but, most of all, because in the case of a request for a blocked vote, the government does not have to run the risk of having to resign, which is the classic downside to technical confidence. On the other hand, it should be borne in mind that 'technical confidence' in Italy can be required for a series of measures and questions that, despite the limitations imposed by the regulations of the Houses and, especially by art. 116, paragraph 4, of the Rules of Procedure of the Chamber of Deputies, covers far more than government bills, for which it is possible to request a fixed-date vote.

Moreover, Italian-style technical confidence produces the same *bloquant* effect as the French text, since once the question of confidence has been posed, the Chamber is called upon to vote on *that* text, whether proposed by the Government or the floor, in the form originally advanced or amended by the Government or from the floor – with the application of the *call for confidence* produced by the Government, which must resign if rejected by the Assembly.

Compared with these advantages of the technical vote of confidence as it is currently used (and abused) in parliamentary practice, the system of voting at a fixed date would only have gone against the (relative) speeding up of the work of the Chamber regarding the measures considered decisive by the Government and the Government itself, without (as is also the case in France) forcing the resignation of the Government in the event of rejection. It would have been a somewhat minor advantage compared with the *vote bloqué*. If the new text had been approved, at the end of the 'procedure' set out in paragraph 7 of art. 72, the Government might well have found itself faced with a text so amended by parliament that it would have been totally unlike the one 'essential for the implementation of the government programme' that it had brought before the Chamber for examination on a fixed date!

On the basis of these assumptions, it would have been natural to express some doubts. Would the Government have been able to 'withdraw' a bill that it no longer considered *its own* in its new form subsequent to parliamentary debate or at least the request for a vote on a fixed date?

In the light of these considerations and the circumstance that the new text of art. 77 would have imposed stricter limits on the Government's ability to legislate through decree laws in cases of 'necessity and urgency', accepting the reflections that have long been invoked in legal scholarship, it is legitimate to suggest that technical confidence would have continued to be – except in the case of a particular convergence of opinion between Government and the parliamentary majority – an instrument of considerable importance for the Government with all the positive and negative consequences that this always implies. These and other questions were raised by the new regulatory framework regarding the Government's ability to influence the law-making process[78].

Of course, it should be borne in mind that among the negative consequences of such a specious use of parliamentary confidence, aiming to limit the freedom of members of the parliamentary majority, the concept of confidence as the positive and value-adding trust between parties for a common purpose is eroded in public opinion, which is all too often highly critical of the way the institutions, and especially the people who represent them, respect values.

3. - 3.4. A new relationship of confidence

It may be useful, at this point, to examine to what extent the asymmetric bicameralism of the reform constituted a change in the form of parliamentary government envisaged by the 1948 Constitu-

---

[78] A special case would have been the approval of the so-called bicameral laws, which would have preserved the equal roles of the Chamber and Senate. In fact, the incipit of the new text of art. 72 explicitly prohibited the Government from voting on these bills on a certain date, nor would it have been conceivable to pose the so-called 'question of technical confidence' in a branch of Parliament that did not enjoy the confidence of the Government. It would have been legitimate to assume that the Executive would have found itself in a very difficult political situation, in some cases with no way out, especially as among the subjects of bicameral competence there were many potentially central areas for the implementation of the political program of a Government, and in the new framework the Government-Senate relationship had no political connection with the majority, as the composition of the new Senate would have been based on territorial considerations.

tion, and especially the delicate question of parliamentary confidence, the fulcrum of this form of government.

It is immediately evident that only the Chamber, being directly elected by the electoral body and renewed by election on a fixed basis, would have been the organ of political legitimation and, as such, would have endowed political legitimacy upon the Government and, ultimately, all the institutional activity of the State. The new text of art. 55 para. 2 stated very clearly that the Nation is represented solely by the individual members of parliament ('Each member of the Chamber of Deputies represents the Nation'), adding in paragraph 3 that only the Chamber of Deputies can express its confidence in the Government.

Paragraph 3 of art. 55 of the revised text stated that '*The Chamber of Deputies shall express its confidence in the Government and exercises political guidance, the legislative function, and that of overseeing the Government's activities*'. Clearly, then, it is not just a Chamber that can confer a vote of confidence; it is *the only one* with the right to do so, by virtue, of course, of being elected directly by the people. The new law also conferred upon the Chamber the function of political guidance, as well as the legislative functions and oversight of Government. The Chamber did not have the sole prerogative over the last two, as it did on the matter of expressing confidence, but it did have the *function*, thus leaving room for other subjects with the same functions, in particular the activities of the new Senate of the Republic with its legislative function.

Was it a coincidence that the Chamber, the sole politically legitimating body, saw as its first task that of conferring (or not conferring) confidence on the Government, that is, of ensuring the bond between the principle organ of the central State and the people as the electoral body? And was it mere chance that after this came that of political guidance, to which Government would surely have contributed, helping to bring necessary stability to the country? And was it by sheer chance that the third on the list was the legislative function of the only elected Chamber, a function that in both the classical constitutional systems and the 1948 Constitution was the main, most jealously guarded, and noble function of every Parliament? And that last of all came oversight of the Government's actions?

In effect, this list in art. 55, paragraph 2 requires some reflection. It was observed, in the *opening* of an 'encyclopaedia entry' on parliamentary confidence commenting on art. 94 of the Constitution (then as now the only article in the Italian Constitution to address the topic of confidence), that the article in question prescribed how confidence was to be conferred by the Houses, without stating 'what confidence means'[79]. Of course, there is no doubt that the functions other than confidence listed in paragraph 2 of art. 55 of the Boschi-Renzi reform, on the other hand, may in fact give a specific and very dense meaning to the term. The new political body,

---

[79] M. Carducci, Art. 94, entry in R. Bifulco, A. Celotto, M. Olivetti (ed), *Commentario alla Costituzione*, p.1811 Turin, 2006.

the Chamber of Deputies, had become the mainstay and driving force of the new institutional life of the country, through a set of responsibilities that, starting from confidence, created a very close relationship with the Government, expressed through its guidance and oversight regarding its activity. Lastly, and albeit with a leading role for the Chamber, it had a legislative function. It may be said that, in some way, the power to grant confidence seemed to be a condition for its further functions, which, in turn, looked almost like confirmations of the central importance of the power to grant confidence that constituted more than ever, in the new form that the Italian Parliamentary Republic was to take, the core and the 'fulcrum', on which all the institutional 'forces' would be centred. In fact, the numerical relationship between the Chamber and the Senate evidently ensured that the former had a prominent role in the election of the President of the Republic in joint session; moreover, in the election of the five constitutional judges appointed by Parliament, three would have been appointed by the Chamber and two by the Senate. A further and evident strengthening of the Chamber's role as a political body stemmed from the aforementioned elimination of the areas of legislative competence shared between the State and Regions, and above all from the possibility of asserting the so-called supremacy clause, i.e., the possibility of also approving, upon Government proposal, laws on matters reserved to the competence of the Regions, 'when the protection of the legal or economic unity of the Republic so requires, that is, to protect the national interest' (Article 117, paragraph 3).

Clearly, the wording of the old, and surviving, art. 94 stating that 'the government must receive the confidence of both Houses of Parliament' is very different.

At a time when the decision-making institutions of the Republic are increasingly required to be able and effective in their choices, the reform undoubtedly sought a new representation of political powers that would make it more visible and more immediate, also thanks, as we shall see, to the electoral law proposed by the Government and passed in conjunction with the constitutional reform, and the mutually necessary collaboration between the Chamber of Deputies and the Government of the Republic! Ultimately, this representation is very different from that prescribed in the current Constitution, where the Government appears at a much later stage in the constitutional text (art. 92), isolated from the complex constitutional system in force.

This was a new form of representation that the legislator hoped would be able to renew the now tired metaphor that aimed, in the first Republic, to equate (and in some ways successfully) the Parliament with the People through the proportional electoral system and therefore equated parliamentary confidence with the substantial confidence that the Italian people show in the institutions through the formal institution of parliamentary confidence.

It is as though there was a desire to underline a new alliance rather than a sense of otherness between the Government and the Chamber, in the new times and in the new Constitution, largely coinciding and working together in an increasingly (and necessarily) efficient and increasingly supportive form of governance. The new Constitution seemed to be saying that according to the democratic-majority principle, the Italian people could have confidence in the new representative hendiadys set out in art. 55.

The proposed art. 55 aims, rather, to respond to the new political needs, including those of Italy, so that the direction to take seems to be above all a collaboration between the institutions and the political forces in order to ensure the democratic governability of the country, as well as to 'stay' in the European Community and the international community. This means staying within a community with its effective ability to respond and suggest ways of acting when faced with the many opportunities that present themselves for the interests, and for a significant contribution, of a country like Italy, that does not lack an original culture of its own, including on the political and institutional plane. There is no doubt, as the events between the sixteenth and seventeenth legislature[80] have amply con-

---

[80] After the fall of the Berlusconi Government, which had been overwhelmed by the crisis on the international markets of the so-called spread (the marked differential between the value of Italian government bonds compared with those of other European countries), the 16th legislature (from 2008 to 2013), closed as a 'Presidential Government' chaired by economist Mario Monti. The 17th legislature (2013-2018) saw three governments in succession, starting with a nationally unified majority and ending with a centre-left majority 'reinforced' by substantial changes of political colour by

firmed, that the greater (or weaker) strength of national government makes the Republic more (or less) proactive and credible in the eyes of the community.

Of course, the so-called Boschi-Renzi constitutional reform did not get past the referendum of 4th December 2016, and the reform was rejected by 59.1% of voters[81].

---

members of the centre right. It goes without saying at this point that Italy's political weight on the international level, and especially at Community level, has been greatly affected by this internal instability; perhaps with the sole exception of the period in which the approval of the Boschi-Renzi reform and the apparent solidity of the Renzi government made it possible to imagine greater government stability.

[81] 19,419, 507 NO votes were cast, representing the Italian voters' will to reject constitutional reform against 13,432,208 YES votes, amounting to 65.47% of those entitled to vote.

Chapter IV

A *look at the recent electoral legislation*

4.1. *The so-called Italicum. The electoral law accompanying the Renzi-Boschi Reform*

'Voting is a fundamental tenet of democracy because voting, election and representation are tools without which democracy cannot be achieved'[82]. The importance of the electoral system adopted alongside any modern democratic constitution is therefore obvious.

It is the electoral system itself, in fact, that makes it possible to transform the votes of the electorate into seats in parliament, identifying at the same time which candidates will actually occupy them.

What is more, it is widely known that the type of electoral system adopted strongly conditions the form of government a country has. This is because it determines the type of relationship that is established between the electorate and the various constitutional bodies, and the relationship these have with each other. It is clear just how much influence the electoral system can have on the kind of

---

[82] T.E. Frosini, *Forme di governo e partecipazione popolare*, Turin, 2008, p.23.

leadership that the Government will have, as well as the selection of the people that will be called to carry it out, namely the Head of Government or the President of the Council.

From this stems the importance of the electoral law, i.e., the law that regulates in detail the electoral system adopted by each country. This law is so important that in many modern States the Constitution itself regulates the electoral mechanism: this was the case of the Weimar Republic, as today in Belgium and Spain, for example[83].

The Italian Constitution, on the other hand, established that the electoral system should be governed by ordinary law, clearly making it easier to modify in order to better adapt to changes in the political life of the country. There is, however, a possible negative side, namely that a parliamentary majority, perhaps in the run-up to new elections, may adopt an electoral law thought to favour it.

In any case, the complexity of legislative choice on this matter has meant that changing the electoral law has often proved extremely difficult in Italy, so that even the pure proportional electoral system adopted in 1948, together with the Republican Constitution, lasted almost fifty years and was only set aside after a very cleverly constructed referendum led to the repeal of the 1948 law in 1993[84].

---

[83] For a comparative overview of the relationship between electoral systems and the constitutional order as a whole, see A. Morrone, *Sistema elettorale e ordinamento costituzionale. profili di teoria generale*, in AIC n.3/2017.

[84] The referendum took place on 18 and 19 April 1993 in a broad-ranging referendum which posed eight different questions to the Italian people. The electoral

The fact that, as mentioned above, both the De Mita-Iotti and the D'Alema Commissions, alongside their proposals for constitutional reform, also presented a proposal for an electoral law to be adopted at the same time as the new Constitution, testifies once again to the difficulty of carrying out profound revision of the constitutional framework without also producing a suitable electoral law to go with it.

It is not surprising, therefore, that the Renzi-Boschi constitutional reform was also strategically combined (from the Government's point of view) with a new electoral law, the so-called *Italicum* (Law 52 of 2015). It should be added, however, that, in any case, electoral reform had clearly become necessary following Constitutional Court ruling No. 1 of 2014 declaring the electoral law in force up to that time, the so-called *Porcellum* (Law 270 of 2005), unconstitutional[85].

---

law was promoted by the Radicals and Mario Segni and obtained a largely favourable result to the abrogation of part of the electoral law in force with a percentage of 82.74%. The turnout was also high: 77.01%. Following the referendum, two new electoral laws were passed: n.276/1993, on the election of the Senate of the Republic and law n.277/1993, on the election of the Chamber of Deputies. The electoral system was called *Mattarellum* after its proponent, Sergio Mattarella, President of the Italian Republic at the time of writing. For further information on the history of Italian electoral laws and attempts at reform, see the exhaustive text by F. Clementi, *Vent'anni di legislazione elettorale (1993-2013)* in Rivista Trimestrale di Diritto pubblico, n.2/2015, pp. 557 ff.

[85] This was the electoral law that had regulated the election of the Chamber and Senate in Italy from its approval in 2005 until the Constitutional Court's 2014 decision. The law had been proposed by the centre-right majority, and in particular, by the Minister for Reform, Roberto Calderoli, who had called the law 'pigswill', hence the name of the law: 'Porcellum'. For further details, see A. Pertici, *La sentenza della*

The *Italicum* was based on a possible two-round system with proportional representation, but with a majority bonus going to the party with at least 40% of the votes at the first stage or, if no party reached this figure, the party with the greatest number of votes at a subsequent ballot. The winning party would be awarded, as mentioned, a majority bonus, which would have guaranteed at least the 340 seats necessary to guarantee the ability to govern in the only directly elected House, the Chamber of Deputies. There was no lack of complex and heated debate around the enactment of this law, with authoritative constitutionalists[86] holding opposing views on the constitutionality of the law itself, especially in terms of the criteria of legitimacy for electoral laws as identified in the aforementioned Constitutional Court judgment no. 1/2014, now no longer effective due to the repeal of the law itself.

Within the overall scope of this essay, it may be useful to ask whether the set of reforms proposed by the Renzi government actually constituted a change of the form of government and, in particular, whether it removed the Italian institutional system from

Corte Costituzionale sulla legge elettorale: l'incostituzionalità ingannevole. *Quaderni costituzionali*, 1/2014.

[86] On the theme of unconstitutionality, see G. D'Anna, *Strutturale incostituzionalità e irragionevolezza del ballottaggio*, in Forum Cost., 3 June 2015; V. Onida, *ibid.*; F. Ragusa, *Il perfezionamento imperfetto dei ballottaggi...*, in *Riforme.net*, 9 June 2014; L. Trucco, *Il sistema elettorale Italicum-bis alla prova della sent. Corte cost. n. 1/2014*, in *Consulta online*, 27 April 2015, 285-305; M. Volpi, *Italicum due: una legge elettorale abnorme*, in *Questione giustizia*; on the topic of constitutional consistency, to name a few of the most authoritative, see A. Barbera, *La nuova legge elettorale*, in *Quaderni Costituzionali*, 3/ 2015 p. 645 ff.; T.E. Frosini, *Rappresentanza, Governabilità, Italicum*, testo dell'audizione presso la commissione affari costituzionali della Camera, 15 April 2015, in *Confronti costituzionali*, 12 May 2015.

the form of *rationalised parliamentary government*, weak as it may have been, that the Italian Constituent Assembly had chosen when it passed the famous Perassi[87] motion and that is anchored, as is proper to parliamentary government, in the institution of political and legal confidence. This is certainly a difficult question to answer and, in any case, it would be of merely pleonastic and defining value.

It should be underlined, however, that the so-called *Italicum* tried to frame a system that would allow the electorate to establish the government majority and, indirectly (but much 'less indirectly' than in the previous system), choose the future President of the Council in the person of the leader of the majority party. This characteristic, which, in the opinion of the writer would have been in some way positive, both because it aimed to introduce a majority-based parliamentary system (rather than the compromise-based system typical of Italian political history), and be-

---

[87] The Perassi motion is considered a fundamental moment in Italian constitutional history, the moment when the Constituent Assembly, after heated debate, chose a form of parliamentary government with rationalisation mechanisms meant to guarantee the Executive a certain stability. The motion stated that 'the parliamentary system should be adopted but with constitutional provisions to protect the stability of government operations and prevent the degeneration of parliamentarianism'. It should be added that, in reality, a system of weak rationalisation has in fact emerged, whose mechanisms aiming to achieve this objective are mainly identified in the presence of a President of the Republic who guarantees and acts as political intermediary and, especially, a Constitutional Court endowed with significant powers safeguarding the Constitution itself. For further in-depth analysis, see Matteo Frau, *L'attualità del parlamentarismo razionalizzato*, in *Nomos*, le attualità del diritto, 3/2016; for a reflection on the need for reform on this topic, see M. Volpi (ed), *Istituzioni e sistema politico in Italia: bilancio di un ventennio*, 2015.

cause it would have allowed the electorate to feel more involved in choosing the political figure with greatest 'weight' from within the institutions, especially after a ballot. It was not surprising that some have argued that the 'combined provisions' of the Boschi-Renzi reform and the *Italicum* would have led to a form of premiership.

In any case, if the questions regarding constitutional legitimacy had been urgent from the start, the negative outcome of the constitutional *referendum* rejecting the so-called Renzi-Boschi constitutional reform left some vestiges of a more comprehensive reform project intact. Thus, in the wake of the referendum, questions regarding constitutionality were supplemented by those on the functionality of the so-called *Italicum*, not least because it envisaged the election of only one Chamber rather than both, as in the surviving Italian two-chamber system.

Constitutional Court ruling 35 of 2017 definitively dispelled any doubts by dismantling the fundamental cornerstones of electoral law 52 of 2015, declaring it illegitimate in several places[88]. The

---

[88] More specifically, the main points of illegitimacy identified by the Court regarded the run-off envisaged by the so-called *Italicum*, not in itself, but because the law in question also allowed access to the possible second round by a list that 'had obtained a low result in the first round but nevertheless obtained the bonus, and with it more than double the seats on the basis of the votes obtained in the first round', thus excessively reducing 'the representative nature of the elected assembly'. The other fundamental point in the law criticised by the Constitutional Court was the possibility for blocked front-runners to stand in more than one constituency and to choose only later, at their discretion, the one for election: 'the arbitrary option unreasonably entrusts the fate of the vote of preference cast by the voter in the chosen constituency to the decision of the head of the list, distorting its outcome, in violation not only of the principle of equality, but also of the personal nature of the vote enshrined in articles 3 and 48, second paragraph, of the Constitution'.

Constitutional Court's decision created a truly chaotic scenario, with two different electoral laws for the Chamber and the Senate, applying what was left of the *Italicum* after the judgment to the Chamber, i.e. a proportional system with a majority bonus, while in the Senate, since the *Italicum* contained nothing about election to this House, the purely proportional system arising from the previous electoral law (the so-called Legge Calderoli) remained in force, even if it had been partially censured, as we have seen, by Constitutional Court decision no. 1 of 2014.

In reality, although the Constitutional Court had specified that the electoral law resulting from the combined provisions of these two different laws (the so-called *Consultellum*) was 'subject to immediate application', the Italian lawmakers immediately began working on a new electoral law, starting from the monition contained in Decision no. 35 of 2017, specifying that the Constitution does not in fact prevent the adoption of two different electoral systems for the Chamber of Deputies and the Senate, provided that 'when the results of the elections are known, the systems adopted do not hinder the formation of homogeneous parliamentary majorities', ensuring the ability to govern.

4. - 4.2. *The so-called Rosatellum and the unlikely majorities*

November 3, 2017 saw the publication in the Official Gazette of the new electoral law, the so-called *Rosatellum* bis[89] (Law 165/2017) named after its creator, Ettore Rosato.

This law prescribes identical methods for electing both the Chamber of Deputies and the Senate and constitutes a mixed electoral system (majority and proportional), in which 37% of the deputies and senators are elected in single-member constituencies using a majority system (only one candidate per coalition; the one with the most votes is elected according to the traditional English first-pass-the-post system), 61% are elected from a proportional list system, and the remaining 2% are elected, again according to a proportional system, by Italians resident abroad. The proportional seats in the Senate are allocated on a regional basis and on a national basis in the Chamber. The *Rosatellum*, unlike the *Italicum*, which envisages individual lists, reintroduces coalitions, so that several lists can join forces. For this reason, the latter can indicate only one candidate for a single-member district, but they can submit different lists for the purposes of proportional distribution[90]. According to the in-

---

[89] The term 'bis' is used here because there was a previous version of the same law, proposed by the same Ettore Rosato. It was very similar to the one that was approved but with a different proportion between the majority and proportional quotas (50 and 50) and a different threshold of exclusion (5%). The law supported by the Democratic Party and the Northern League was abandoned because it lacked sufficient parliamentary support.

[90] More specifically, the vote given to one of the lists of the coalition, with or without indicating the majority candidate, will not only benefit the individual candidate in terms of proportional distribution, but also the list that has been voted for. If,

dications contained in Constitutional Court judgment no. 1/2014, these must be shortlists so that, at least in theory, voters can know the candidates for whom they will be voting[91], even if they are not able to choose between them through a preference mechanism, as these lists are 'blocked'[92].

What, then, are the legislator's aims with the new law? And what are the chances that the *Rosatellum* can actually achieve them? The *Rosatellum* famously represents the achievement of a very difficult compromise between the political forces in Parliament, even beyond the parliamentary majority itself[93]. For these reasons, it does not constitute, as in the case of the *Italicum*, a clear and precise selection by the legislator from among the possible ways of

on the other hand, the voter votes directly for an individual candidate in a coalition, without indicating the list, the vote goes to the coalition and, therefore, its 'weight' will be distributed among the coalised lists in proportion to the votes gained by each of them in that constituency.

[91] In order to comply with the content of decision no. 1/2014 of the Court, which had censured the practice of multi-member constituencies with very broad, blocked lists, which would have been detrimental to the principle of representation (Art. 49 Cost.), a new division of the territory into constituencies was carried out. In no multi-member constituency may the list of candidates exceed 4, in compliance with the principle of gender alternation; the subject matter delegated to the Government through the electoral law is established by the Legislative Decree of 12 December 2017 n.189.

[92] The thresholds of exclusion are fixed at 10% for the coalitions, provided that at least one of their lists reaches the threshold of 3% at national level. Any lists that do not reach at least 1% do not count towards the percentage in favour of the coalition of which they are part. The threshold for the lists outside a coalition is 3%: reaching this threshold allows lists from coalitions below the 10 % threshold to participate in the allocation of seats at national level.

[93] The law was supported by both the Government majority parties of the centre left (Democratic Party), but also by the centre-right forces (Forza Italia, Lega Nord, Alleanza Popolare). It was strongly opposed by the Progressive Democratic Movement and the Five Star Movement.

translating the will of the electorate into parliamentary seats and consequent political leadership, but it is a sort of overlapping of the different political and electoral requirements in the need to find, in a short time, a compromise that would allow Italian citizens to go to the polls following an electoral law that at least has the merit of not prescribing totally different mechanisms for the two Chambers.

Of course, when preparing an electoral law, the legislator should aim to strike a balance between two main objectives: representativeness on the one hand and governability on the other. If, from the point of view of representativeness, the proportional component is clearly prevalent, albeit without the possibility of attributing preferences to individual candidates, it can anyway be said that it has been taken into account. Concerning the power to govern, as already noted, the need to find a necessary compromise between the various political forces has led to this objective being sidelined.

In the current essentially tripartite Italian political scenario, it appears unlikely that the objective of an absolute majority in the two branches of Parliament, and therefore, of the ability to govern, can be reached through a single, homogeneous list. In reality, it is also unlikely to be reached by coalitions, which, due to the lack of uniformity among the various forces making them up, are not expected to be able to ensure a homogeneous and, above all, lasting lead[94].

Basically, it looks as though the regulatory framework envisaged by this electoral law could give rise to scenarios already familiar in Italian politics, namely Governments struggling to hold their own, a phenomenon that marked almost the entire so-called 'Second Republic', where governments resulting from electoral coalitions were formed at the beginning of the legislature, followed later by so-called Presidential Governments, tasked with seeking new parliamentary balances maintained by new *leaders* to ensure the continuity of the legislature[95].

In the far-from-remote eventuality that no list or coalition is able to constitute a parliamentary majority able to ensure trust in the Government, one would be faced with a situation that is already known, but even more evident in the history of Italian politics: the subsequent search for a parliamentary majority among political forces that had clashed during the electoral phase, a situation already typical of the so-called First Republic.

Another consideration comes to mind at this point: the relative acquiescence of the Italian electorate regarding the formation of coalition governments *after* the elections, typical, as we have men-

---

[94] In this sense, see the very recent A. Martines, 'Il minotauro 2.0'. l'incerto equilibrio tra rappresentatività e governabilità nel Rosatellum bis, in Forum di Quaderni Costituzionali, 25 February 2018.

[95] On this, see P. Lauvaux E A. Le Divellec, *Les grandes démocraties contemporaines*, Paris, 2015.

tioned, of the so-called First Republic, rested on at least two circumstances. The first was that such coalitions were formed between relatively similar forces, where, around the Christian Democrats, a leading and inter-class party, rotated minor forces belonging to the liberal or reformist tradition, while the two radical parties of the right and left, of which the most important was most certainly the Communist Party, remained in constant opposition. Secondly, this consolidated political practice had led to a culture among the electorate that was in some way predisposed to consider it endemic to the democratic system, and probably because there existed a different climate of trust at the time between the electorate and the political class.

In short, in this scenario it is easy to imagine that, from the electorate's point of view, citizens would soon find themselves face to face with Governments supported by parliamentary alliances formed by parties that had sworn they would never have worked together, and most probably also with initially wholly unimagined leaders. If we reflect on the fact that, as mentioned above, a very important role in post-electoral scenarios will be played by a President of the Republic who is not directly elected by the people, it is easy to imagine that Italian citizens will be under the impression of having a political class actually disconnected from the electorate, one that decides the fate of the country within its own circuit.

In a situation like this, the already difficult relationship between governors and the governed risks becoming even more

strained. It should be recalled that since the watershed of the beginning of the Second Republic, Italian citizens have felt a greater
need to use the vote to gain greater influence on political and government equilibria, also aiming to choose the coalitions most apt to
govern and, above all, a President of the Council from among those
proposed by the various political forces during the election campaign. This has happened in a scenario that is not only Italian, but
probably also global, in which the governed are no longer content
to simply choose the members of a Legislative Assembly – giving
rise, as is typical of the more classical formulation of representative
democracy – to a *democracy of authorisation*, i.e., a political regime
that gives the elected a sort of 'green light' to choose in the name of
the governed but with constraints in terms of mandate or political
leadership.

In a world where decision-making processes have become
complicated and bureaucracies are assuming increasing power, citizens feel the need to establish a face-to-face relationship with their
rulers, a need that tends to catalyse in Italy and elsewhere, towards
the Head of the Executive[96]. In fact, it is this figure that provides the
best response to a social need for the attribution, and therefore the

---

[96] It is no coincidence that there was real talk of a global presidentialisation
movement – see T. Pouguntke and P. Webb, *The Presidentialization of Politics: A
Comparative Study of Modern Democracies*, Oxford University Press, 2005. The study,
which analyses the cases of 14 countries in comparative terms, shows that governments
tend to follow a presidential logic, mainly from three points of view, through 1) an increase in the power and autonomy of the executive; 2) an increase in the autonomy of
the executive power from political parties; 3) the emergence of electoral processes focused on leadership.

assumption, of responsibility by at least the 'man in government', and the transparency and clarity of the institutions and decision-making mechanisms. This would give rise to a sort of 're-appropriation' of politics by the citizenry, moving towards the creation of an investiture democracy, also rebuilding faith in politics that is so lacking today, and of which the abstention figures constitute an obvious indicator[97].

If this is true, the new electoral law, the so-called *Rosatellum*, despite being the result of a very complicated balance, and being approved by a broad majority does not, all things considered, seem to answer the need for new policy that the Italians seem to desire. It is most likely that after the elections we will continue to witness what the Italian political world itself calls 'the theatre of politics', a sort of spectacle in which the various leaders 'stage' a public debate that does not seem, however, to reflect the actual balances between them, a situation for which Italian public opinion has coined the caustic and telling term *'inciucio'* (obscure power sharing)[98].

It does not seem, at this point, to be an exaggeration to conclude that after the failure of many attempts at reform and the shipwreck of the last attempt by the Renzi government, the Italian polit-

[97] See the exhaustive studies of Pierre Rosanvallon on changes in modern democracy and the crisis of political representation, namely: *La démocratie inachevée*, Paris, 2000; *La contre-démocratie, la politique à l'age de la défiance*, Seuil, 2006; *La légitimité démocratique*, Seuil, 2008; *Le Bon Gouvernement*, Seuil, 2015

[98] A term borrowed from Neapolitan dialect that has long been used in the description of Italian political scenarios to refer to an informal agreement between political forces of opposing ideologies which, it is believed, set in motion a sort of *do ut des*, or a real division of power.

ical system has remained in a sort of gridlock between a Constitution now in its seventieth year and certainly ripe for change, and a multiplicity of projects desirous of shaping a new order, wrought by a political class too divided and too focused on its own interests to produce a new institutional synthesis capable of meeting the expectations of at least the majority of Italian citizens, from those different plans.

Attempts at reform, with new bills or bicameral commissions like those that have marked the last thirty years of the life of the Italian Republic will most likely not come to an end. It is legitimate to assume that the *Rosatellum bis* – despite the traditional Latin ending found in the names of all Italian electoral laws, often with a rather more derisory than descriptive tone (*Mattarellum, Porcellum, Italicum, Consultellum*) – is hardly likely to become a permanent feature of Italian political life.[99]

> *The elections of 4 March, 2018, which took place during the review phase of the drafts of this essay, constituted the first 'dry run' of the so-called* Rosatellum *law. The election results have, in fact, confirmed the forecasts and assumptions made in the course of this study, in particular with regard to the ability to form a government. In fact, none of the political forces involved have reached the minimum threshold of 40% that would have*

[99] As soon as it was passed, S. Ceccanti defined the Rosatellum as a 'bridge electoral law'. See Cfr. S. Ceccanti, *Legislazione elettorale. Italia. Una nuova legge ponte nella transizione che prosegue*, a transcription of a contribution presented at the *Convegno della Societé de Législation comparé* and the *Centre d'études consttutionnel et politiques* at the University of Paris II '*La loi électorale en Europe*', Paris, 10 November 2017.

guaranteed the winning list or coalition a majority in Parliament. At this point, of course, it is necessary to form a majority greater than that of the coalition or list presented during the election campaign or alternatively, and more predictably, the formation of a so-called Presidential Government or Government of Experts able to lead the country towards a new electoral law ... again.

Short Bibliography

A: Di Giovine, *Note sulla legge costituzionale n.1/1997*, in *Quad. Cost.* 1/1997;

Anzon Deming A., *La nuova strada per le riforme, non illegittima ma rischiosa*, in Rivista AIC 3/2013;

Anzon Demmig A., *Perché non convincono le ragioni del no al referendum costituzionale*, in Rivista AIC, n.2/2016;

Armaroli P., *L'introvabile governabilità. Le strategie istituzionali dei partiti dalla Costituente alla Commissione* Bozzi, Padova, 1986;

Barbera A., *La nuova legge elettorale*, in *Quaderni Costituzionali*, 3/2015

Barbera A., *Una riforma per la Repubblica*, Roma, 1991;

Bin R., *Cercasi ragioni serie per il no*, in Rivista AIC 3/2016

Bonfiglio S., *Sulla rigidità delle Costituzioni. Il dibattito italiano e la prospettiva comparata*, in *Diritto pubblico*, n.1/2015;

Brunelli G., *La funzione legislativa bicamerale nel testo di revisione costituzionale: profili problematici*, in *Rassegna parlamentare* 4/2015

Calamandrei P., *Costruire la democrazia. Premessa alla Costituente*, 1945, Milano;

Caravale G., *Il Governo legislatore. Esecutivo ed attività normativa in Gran Bretagna e negli Stati Uniti*, Milano, 2004;

Carducci M., Art. 94, entry in R. Bifulco, A. Celotto, M. Olivetti (eds), *Commentario alla Costituzione*, Torino, 2006;

Carnevale P., *Considerazione critiche sull'iter e sulla procedura referendaria*, in *federalismi.it*, n. 12, 2016;

Carnevale P., *La revisione costituzionale nella prassi del terzo millennio, una rassegna problematica*, in Rivista AIC, 1/2013, p. 24 ff.

Cherchi R., *La forma di governo: dall'Assemblea costituente alle prospettive di revisione costituzionale*, in *Costituzonalismo.it*, 30/12/2008;

Cicconetti S. M., *Revisione Costituzionale*, entry in Enciclopedia del diritto, Milano, vol. XL, 1989;

Clementi F., *Vent'anni di legislazione elettorale (1993-2013)* in Rivista Trimestrale di Diritto pubblico, n.2/2015;

Cuocolo L., *I 'maxi-emendamenti' tra opportunità e legittimità costituzionale*, in Giurisprudenza costituzionale, n.6/2004;

D'Anna G., *Strutturale incostituzionalità e irragionevolezza del ballottaggio*, in Forum Cost., June 2015;

De Giovanni B., *Elogio della sovranità politica*, Napoli, 2015;

De Vergottini G., *Referendum e revisione costituzionale una analisi comparata* in Giurisprudenza costituzionale, n.2/1994;

Dickmann R., *Appunti sul ruolo del Senato nel nuovo Parlamento repubblicano*, in Federalismi.it, n. 3/2016;

Dogliani M., *Potere costituente e revisione costituzionale della lotta per la Costituzione*, in A.A.V.V., *Il futuro della Costituzione*, Torino, 1996;

Faraguna P., *Ai confini della Costituzione. Principi supremi e identità costituzionale*, Milano, 2015;

Fedele P. (ed) Revisione, in Grande dizionario enciclopedico, XV, Torino, 1971;

Ferrajoli L., *Democrazia e Costituzione*, in *Il futuro della Costituzione*;

Ferri G., *Il referendum nella revisione costituzionale*, Padova, 2001;

Fontana G.P., *Il referendum costituzionale nei processi di riforma della Repubblica*, Napoli, 2013;

Frau M., *L'attualità del parlamentarismo razionalizzato*, in *Nomos, le attualità del diritto*, 3/2016;

Frosini T. E, *Potere costituzionale e sovranità popolare* in *Rassegna Parlamentare*, n.7, 2016;

Frosini T. E., *Forme di governo e partecipazione popolare*, Torino, 2008, III edizione;

Frosini T.E., *Rappresentanza, Governabilità, Italicum*, testo dell'audizione presso la commissione affari costituzionali della Camera, 15 April 2015, in *Confronti costituzionali*, 12 May 2015;

Fusaro C., *Per una storia delle riforme istituzionali (1948-2015)*, in *Rivista Trimestrale di Diritto pubblico*, n.2/2015;

Galeotti S., *La Garanzia Costituzionale*, Milano 1950;

Gallo F., *Possibilità e limiti della revisione costituzionale*, in *Quaderni costituzionali* 3/2013;

Lauvaux P. e Le Divellec A., *Les grandes démocraties contemporaines*, Paris, Puf, 2015;

Lijphart A., *Le democrazie contemporanee*, Bologna, 2002;

Luhmann Niklas, La fiducia, Bologna, 2002;

Lupo N., *Emendamenti, maxi-emendamenti e questione di fiducia nelle legislature del maggioritario* in Gianfrancesco E.. e Lupo N. (eds), *Le regole del diritto* parlamentare nella dialettica tra maggioranza e opposizione, Luiss University Press, Roma, 2007

Luther, J. Portinaro P., Zagrebelsky G. (ed), Il futuro della Costituzione, Torino, 1996;

M. Dogliani, Potere costituente e revisione costituzionale, in Quaderni Costituzionali, 31/1995;

Martines A., 'Il minotauro 2.0'. l'incetto equilibrio tra rappresentatività e governabilità nel Rosatellum bis, in Forum di Quaderni Costituzionali, 25 February 2018;

Mastromarino A., Alcune prime riflessioni (sparse e brevi) in merito al progetto di superamento del bicameralismo paritario, in Focus riforma Costituzionale, Federalismi n.5/2016;

Modugno F., I principi costituzionali supremi come parametro del giudizio di legittimità costituzionale, in Il principio di unità del controllo sulle leggi nella giurisprudenza della Corte costituzionale, Torino, 1991;

Morrone A., Sistema elettorale e ordinamento costituzionale. profili di teoria generale, in AIC n.3/2017;

Mortati C., Istituzioni d Diritto pubblico, Padova,1976;

Olivetti M., La questione di fiducia nel sistema parlamentare italiano, Milano, 1996;

Orlando Vittorio Emanuele, Studio intorno alla forma di governo vigente in Italia secondo la Cost. del 1948 in Rivista trimestrale di diritto pubblico, 1/1951;

Pace A., Costituzioni flessibili e rigide, 1998;

Pace A., I limiti alla revisione costituzionale nell'ordinamento italiano ed europeo, in Nomos. Le attualità del diritto, 1/2016

Pace A., Le insuperabili criticità della riforma costituzionale Renzi-Boschi, in www.libertaegiustizia.it, 25/2/2016;

Pace A., Potere costituente, rigidità costituzionale, autovincoli legislativi, Padova, 2002;

Panunzio S. P., *Riforme costituzionali e referendum*, in *Quaderni Costituzionali*, 3/1990;

Pegoraro L., Rinella A., *Legislazione e procedimento formativo della legge nella proposta di revisione costituzionale*, in *Rassegna Parlamentare*, 1/1998;

Perché Sì, le ragioni della riforma costituzionale, Bari, 2016;

Pertici A., *La sentenza della Corte Costituzionale sulla legge elettorale: l'incostituzionalità ingannevole*. *Quaderni costituzionali*, 1/2014.

Piazza M., *I limiti della revisione costituzionale nell'ordinamento italiano*, Padova, 2002;

Piccirilli G., *Paradossi della questione di fiducia ai tempi del maggioritario*, in *Quaderni Costituzionali*, 2008;

Pisicchio P., *Dal Parlamento legislatore al parlamento degli atti di indirizzo*, in www.forumcostituzionale;

Pouguntke T. and Webb P., *The Presidentialization of Politics: A Comparative Study of Modern Democraties*, Oxford University Press, 2005;

Ragusa F., *Il perfezionamento imperfetto dei ballottaggi...*, in Riforme.net, June 2014;

Ridolfi A., *L'introduzione del voto bloccato*, in AIC Osservatorio costituzionale, 3/2014;

Rosanvallon P., *La contre.démocraite, la politique à l'age de la défiance*, Seuil, 2006;

Rosanvallon P., *La dèmocratie inachevée*, Gallimard, 2000;

Rosanvallon P., *La légitimité démocratique*, Seuil, 2008;

Rosanvallon P., *Le Bon Gouvernement*, Seuil, 2015;

Rossi E., *Il procedimento legislativo delle leggi 'monocamerali': prime considerazioni*, in Rivista AIC 3/2016,

S. Ceccanti, *Legislazione elettorale. Italia. Una nuova legge ponte nella transizione che prosegue*, trascrizione dell'intervento nell'ambito del Convegno della Società de Lègislation comparé e del Centre d'études constiutionnel et politiques dell'Università Paris II 'La loi électorale en Europe', Parigi 10 November 2017;

Salerno G. M., *I referendum in Italia: fortune e debolezze di uno strumento multifunzionale*, in Diritto pubblico comparato ed europeo, 3/2005;

Salerno G.M., *Il disegno di legge costituzionale sull'istituzione del Comitato parlamentare per le riforme costituzionali e elettorali: spunti per alcune riflessioni preliminari*, in Osservatorio costituzionale 00/2013, p. 1 ff.

Sartori G., *Democrazia e definizioni*, Bologna, 1957

Sartori G, *Ingegneria costituzionale comparata. Strutture incentivi ed esiti*, Bologna, 1995

Scoppola P., *La Repubblica dei partiti. Evoluzione e crisi di un sistema politico, 1945-1996*, Bologna, 1997;

Silvestri G., *Il potere costituente come problema teorico giuridico*, in Studi in onore di Leopoldo Elia, II, Milano, 1999;

Staiano S., *Costituzionalisti e popolo*, in federalismi.it, 25/2013;

Traversa S., *In vista del referendum costituzionale: luci ed ombre della riforma*, in Rassegna parlamentare, 2/2016;

Trucco L., *Il sistema elettorale Italicum-bis alla prova della sent. Corte cost. n. 1/2014*, in Consulta online, 27 April 2015;

Urbinati N., *Renzi il plebiscito per non spiegare la verità* in Libertà e Giustizia 25/4/2016 in www.libertaegiustizia.it;

Volpi M. (ed), *Istituzioni e sistema politico in Italia: bilancio di un ventennio*, 2015;

Volpi M., *Italicum due: una legge elettorale abnorme, in Questione giustizia; sul versante della coerenza costituzionale*, X Zagrebelesky G., *Il Crucifige e la democrazia*, Torino, 1995

www.ingramcontent.com/pod-product-compliance
Lightning Source LLC
Chambersburg PA
CBHW071607200326
41519CB00021BB/6912